Aetas Manjurica 14

AETAS MANJURICA

Serie italo-tedesco-russa di studi mancesi
Deutsch-italienisch-russische Studienreihe zur Mandschuforschung
Немецко-итало-русская серия по маньчжуроведению

adiuvantibus

Herbert Franke · Piero Corradini (†) · Veronika Veit
Tatjana A. Pang

ediderunt

Martin Gimm · Giovanni Stary · Michael Weiers

TOMUS 14

2010
Harrassowitz Verlag · Wiesbaden
in Kommission

Tatjana A. Pang / Giovanni Stary

Manchu *versus* Ming
Qing Taizu Nurhaci's "Proclamation"
to the Ming Dynasty

2010
Harrassowitz Verlag · Wiesbaden
in Kommission

Bibliografische Information Der Deutschen Bibliothek:
Die Deutsche Bibliothek verzeichnet diese Publikation in der Deutschen
Nationalbibliografie; detaillierte bibliografische Daten sind im Internet
über https://dnb.dnb.de abrufbar.

Bibliographic information published by Die Deutsche Bibliothek:
Die Deutsche Bibliothek lists this publication in the Deutsche
Nationalbibliografie; detailed bibliographic data is available in the
Internet at https://dnb.dnb.de.

Harrassowitz Verlag, Kreuzberger Ring 7c-d, 65205 Wiesbaden
produktsicherheit.verlag@harrassowitz.de
For further information about the Harrassowitz publishing program consult our
website https://www.harrassowitz-verlag.de

© By the authors
This work, including all of its parts, is protected by copyright.
Any use beyond the limits of copyright law without the permission
of the authors and editors is forbidden and subject to penalty. This applies
particularly to reproductions, translations, microfilms and storage
and processing in electronic systems.
Printed on permanent/durable paper.

ISSN 0931-282X
ISBN 978-3-447-06160-5

Contents

Foreword	VII
Introduction	IX
New facts	XIII
The Manchu and Chinese text	1
Abbreviations and works cited	66

Foreword

In our facsimile-publication of the blockprint "Guimet 61626" (*New Light on Manchu Historiography and Literature*, Wiesbaden: Harrassowitz 1998), we have proposed that it might possibly be the Manchu version of a Chinese xylograph known as *Hou Jin xi Ming Wanli huangdi wen* 後金檄明萬曆皇帝文 – "Proclamation of the Latter Jin to the Ming Wanli Emperor".

To test the validity of our theory we undertook further research in the National Library of China in Beijing, where we were able to check the Chinese original, in the Academia Sinica in Taipei and other Institutions in China, Europe and the United States. In addition, our study included a detailed comparison of relevant Manchu sources, in particular of the *Jiu Manzhou dang* 舊滿洲檔.

We now publish the conclusions of our recent research together with, as far as is possible, a word for word translation of the Manchu and Chinese versions.

Introduction

The title "Proclamation of the Latter Jin to the Ming Wanli Emperor" is purely conventional. It is used in the catalogue of the Beijing State Library, *Beijing tushuguan shanben shumu* 北京圖書館善本書目 (Beijing 1959) to describe this Chinese xylograph. Both the Chinese and Manchu work are without title. Imanishi Shunjū 今西春秋, who edited the Chinese text in facsimile in his article "«Kō Kin geki Min Banreki kōtei bun» ni tsuite 後金檄明萬曆皇帝文について", *Chōsen gakuhō* 朝鮮學報 67 (1973), pp. 137–158,[1] adopted the above-mentioned catalogue entry, and this title was then also used in a reprint in simplified characters published in Pan Zhe 潘喆, Sun Fangming 孫方明, Li Hongbin 李鴻彬 (eds.), *Qing ruguan qian shiliao xuanji* 清入關前史料選輯, vol. 1, Peking 1984, pp. 289–296. As a conventional designation, this title is also used by Qiao Zhizhong 喬治忠, "«Hou Chin xi Ming Wanli huangdi wen» kaoxi 《后金檄明萬曆皇帝文》考析 (*Qingshi yanjiu* 清史研究 3 (1992), pp. 106–110, who however suggested (p. 109) the alternative titles *Hou Jin xi Mingchao wen* 后金檄明朝文 ("Proclamation of the Latter Jin to the Ming Dynasty") or *Nuerhachi xi Mingchao wen* 努爾哈赤檄明朝文 ("Nurhaci's Proclamation to the Ming Dynasty"). A brief description is also found in the 7th volume of the encyclopaedia *Aixin Jueluo jiazu quanshu* 愛新覺羅家族全書, (ed. by Zhang Yuxing 張玉興 et al.), Jilin 1997, pp. 36–37.

The definition "Proclamation" *with reference to the Wanli Emperor*, is clearly wrong. In the "Opening paragraph" the death of the Emperor, together with his son, is mentioned. This excludes the possibility that the document could be addressed to him. Indeed, Nurhaci always accused the "Southern Dynasty" in the Chinese version, which is changed to "You, the Chinese" with a simple *si nikan* in the Manchu text.

---

[1] German translation without facsimile: "Über einen Aufruf der Späteren Chin an die Ming von ca. 1623", *Oriens Extremus* 20/1 (1973), pp. 27–37.

Wanli's son Taichang 泰昌 died on 26th September, 1620, and this justifies Imanishi Shunjū's dating ("around 1623") of the two documents. It is however questionable if the Chinese version was distributed among Chinese officials in order to persuade them of the Ming dynasty's unworthy reign and the consequent imminent loss of the Mandate of Heaven[2] in favour to Nurhaci, even if this statement is found at the end of the "Résumé" according to our subdivision of the text. The whole work, both the Manchu and Chinese versions, gives rather the impression of being a *literary* compilation, based on Nurhaci's utterances as recorded in the *Jiu Manzhou dang* (JMZD), rather than a propagandistic tool for immediate and practical use. The *literary* background is also seen in the manuscript Guimet 61625,[3] in which the orthography, in old Manchu script, shows considerable convergences with the xylograph. A literary background would also justify the parallel compilation of the Manchu version, which was not needed for *propaganda purposes* among the Jurchen (and even Mongol) followers of Nurhaci. This also could explain why the invitation to make the contents known to "the superiors" is found in the Chinese version only.

The content itself, Nurhaci's historical and philosophical utterances, is sometimes found in condensed form in several entries found in the *JMZD*, where in at least three documents his thoughts are explained in messages sent to different addressees.[4] Particularly interesting is the final part of the document from April 1623, since we find here – and this is the only case – the wrong name of the founder of the Ming dynasty, Zhu Yuanzhang, given as Zhu Yuanlong. Since the same mistake is also repeated in the 14th example (see the explanation there in footnote 1 to the "Comment"), we may consider it as a further element for dating the xylograph, which confirms its suggested compilation in or around

---

2   On this well-known aspect of Chinese philosophy see, with reference to Nurhaci, Song Dexuan 宋德宣, *Manzu zhexue sixiang yanjiu* 滿族哲學思想研究, Shenyang 1994, esp. pp. 109–120, and A. M. Martynov & T. A. Pang, "About Ideology of the Early Qing Dynasty", in *Archiv Orientální* 71 (2003), pp. 385–394.

3   Facsimile edition in Pang/Stary 1998, pp. 54–195.

4   See the entry in I, 529 ff / 18th May 1620; II, 1124 ff / 26th May 1622; V, 2040 ff / April 1623).

1623. Noteworthy is also a speech by Nurhaci in February 1626 found in the *Daicing gurun-i fukjin doro neihe bodogon-i bithe*, the "Strategical Plans of the Foundation of the Daicing Dynasty",[5] which – with reference to his philosophical thoughts[6] – sounds like a résumé of the (already compiled?) proclamation:

> "Reading the ancient and contemporary books (*julge te-i bithe*), it is seen that even in great empires the state order is collapsing when its days are numbered and the ruler and the dignitaries are becoming ill and blind; and that even small kingdoms are starting to flourish and the Great *Dao* is growing all the time, when good omens appear one after another, when people and things are thriving well and prospering richly. Now in the Ming empire bad omens are appearing constantly, the emperor and the dignitaries are not taking ther responsibilities to govern seriously and are committing sins against Heaven. Is it then possible to believe in the flaunted power of a Great Imperial Army?"

As concerns the author(s), we suggested in our facsimile edition three names: the lettered Hife († 1652), who "was versed in Mongol and Chinese as well as in Manchu, and served Nurhaci in a literary capacity"[7], and Dahai (1599–1632), who already in Nurhaci's times started the translation of the "Tongjian";[8] he was therefore an expert in ancient

---

5   Blockprint of 1789, chapter VIII, p. 40a; the work is better known with the Chinese title *Huang Qing kaiguo fanglue* 皇清開國方略, which has been translated into German by Erich Hauer, *Huang-Ts'ing K'ai-kuo Fang-lüeh. Die Gründung des mandschurischen Kaiserreiches.* Berlin-Leipzig 1926.
6   For an analysis of Nurhaci's "Chinese sources", among them the *Shujing* 書經, see Pang Xiaomei 龐曉梅 [T. A. Pang], "The Manchu-Chinese text of the 'Proclamation of Nurhaci to the Ming': what version was written first?", in Zhu Chengru 朱誠如 (ed.), *Qingshi lunji. Qinghe Wang Zhonghan jiaoshou jiushi huadan* 清史論集・慶賀王鍾翰教授九十華誕, Beijing 2003, pp. 709–714.
7   A. W. Hummel (ed.), *Eminent Chinese of the Ch'ing Period (1644–1912)*, Washington 1943–1944, p. 663.
8   See T. A. Pan [Pang] "Nachodka konca XX veka: samyj rannij man'čžurskij ksilograf", *Altaica* 4 (2000), pp. 91–100 (esp. 95–96), and Pang Xiaomei 龐曉梅 & G. Sidali 斯達理, "Zui zhongyao kexue faxian zhi yi: Lao Manwen xie de «Hou Jin xi Ming Wanli huangdi wen»" 最重要科發現之

Chinese history and could have discussed it with Nurhaci, who with reference to these historical examples always states that he "heard" about it (from Dahai?). And this is in contrast with the examples from Aisin/Jin (Jurchen) history, which he claimed to have "read". The third "candidate" could be Kūrcan baksi († 1633), a close collaborator of Dahai and head of the "Historiographical Office" – *Kooli ejere bithei yamun*.[9]

一：老滿文寫的《后金檄明萬曆皇帝文》, in Yan Chongnian 閻 崇 年 (ed.), *Manxue yanjiu* 滿 學 研 究 6, Beijing 2000, 186–191. On the "Tongjian" see also W. Fuchs, *Beiträge zur Mandjurischen Bibliographie und Literatur*, Tôkyô 1936, p. 40 and 44.

9   B.-M. Linke, *Zur Entwicklung des mandjurischen Khanats zum Beamtenstaat*, Wiesbaden 1982, p. 230: "historiographische Behörde".

New facts for a revision of the authorship and compilation date

The arguments set out above are however undermined by a hitherto neglected *handwritten* copy of this work, two pages of which have been published under "Lao Manwen shangyu" 老滿文上諭 in *Wenxian congbian* 文獻叢編 2 (1937):[10]

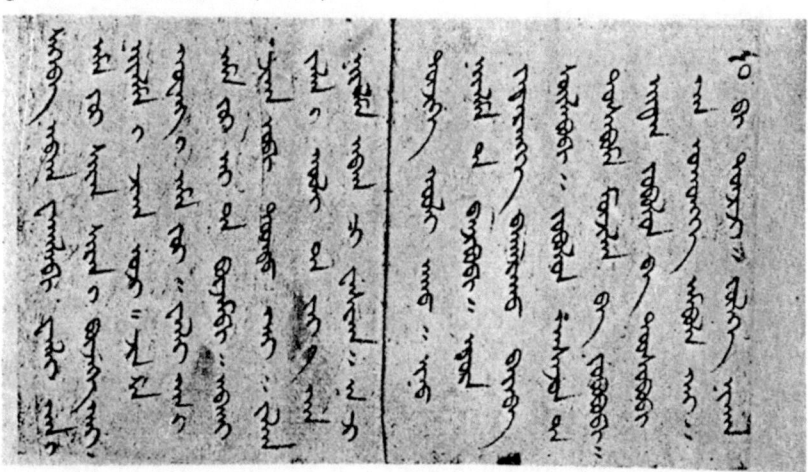

[1] sehebe abka wakalabi wanli han-i
[2] ama jui siran siran-i būc̣ehe kai.
[3] niẙalma-i c̣iha oc̣i: c̣in še
[4] hōwang-i ama jui: wanli han-i
[5] ama jui ai de būc̣embi: abkai
[6] c̣iha obi tuttu kai: jalan
[7] jalan-i kooli de ẙai-a han
[8] niẙalma abka ci wasika: na c̣i

[9] // tūc̣ike kooli akō: inu
[10] niẙalma de banjibubi: eture
[11] jeterengge baharakō beẙebe
[12] sūilabubi: jobolon gasac̣un de
[13] dosabume mūjilen be jobobubi:
[14] eiten jobolon be doosobubi
[15] han ohongge ambula kai:
[16] ○ bi donjic̣i: jūlge nikan

---

10 Reprint Taipei 1964, vol. *shang* 上, p. 82, photo 1, and vol. *xia* 下, p. 1053–1054, comment. This note has been mentioned also by W. Fuchs in his article "Neue Beiträge zur mandjurischen Bibliographie und Literatur", in *Monumenta Serica* VII (1942), pp. 1–37 [on p. 36]. The two specimens have been reprinted in *Sekai bunkashi daikei* 世界文化史大系 vol. 19, Tōkyō 1938, p. 16, without comment.

The photo reproduces half of p. 10, starting from the middle of the third line, the whole of p. 11, and half of the first line of p. 12 of the Guimet xylograph. Inscribed on the cover in old Manchu writing were the words *Mucengge baksi* and a similar script *Mucengge baksi araha* ("written by Mucengge baksi") appeared at the end of the text.

The anonymous report in the *Wenxian congbian* defined the manuscript as a *Qing Taizu banji guanqi beizi zhi shangyu* 清太祖頒給管旗貝子之上諭, "Imperial decree of Qing Taizu promulgated to the princes in charge of the Banners". The contents correspond to the xylograph, as seen from the list of arguments subdivided (as explicitly told) into 19 "patterns" (*ze* 則). The obviously later addition *gūsai beise Šang-šan* was found on the last page, written in reformed Manchu script.

At present, it must be considered lost, at least judging from the fruitless researches carried out in the First National Archives of China (Beijing) and the Academia Sinica (Taipei). According to the *Wenxian congbian*, it was kept in the 1930s in the *Neige daku* 內閣大庫. In his study of the *Chinese* version, Qiao Zhizhong briefly dwelt upon the notice given in the *Wenxian congbian*, interpreting the addition of "Šang-šan" as indicating that the manuscript belonged to his family's property, but ignoring totally and incomprehensibly the references to Mucengge.

The author of this literary work should therefore be "Mucengge", but this meagre information is of little help in reaching a more precise and definite historical and biobibliographical identification of the author. Any conclusion can therefore be only tentative, being based on an unverifiable notice published in 1937. We cannot exclude *a priori* that Mucengge was a simple copyist of the text, and not its author. According to the available sources, the only Mucengge who comes into question is the *mujilen bahabukū* [11] of the Ministry of War created in 1631.[12] and he reappears as *hashū ergi ashan-i amban* ("left vice-president") of the same ministry after its reorganisation in 1638.[13] His name

---

11 Title of an officer in early Qing ministries ranking after the *ashan-i amban* (*shilang* 侍郎, "vice president") and before the *icihiyara hafan* (*langzhong* 郎中, "departmental director"); the office, usually translated with "Informator", was abolished in 1658.
12 See *Hauer*, p. 259.
13 *Ibid.*, p. 469.

is often mentioned in the *JMZD* as a companion of Dahai[14] and collaborator of Kūrcan,[15] This Mucengge had the title *bithesi* (not *baksi*!), took part in 1627 as Kūrcan's "assistant" in his negotiations with Korea[16] and distinguished himself in military actions and diplomatic missions.[17] It could therefore be very probable that, living in this literary atmosphere, he found time to compose this "proclamation" together with the ms. Guimet 61625 which, in writing form and content, closely resembles our xylograph. If this supposition is accepted there is another clue to help establish the time when the work was compiled: the concluding section relates that there was a fall of honey rain in 1616 and 1617. This phenomenon is registered for the third time only in ms Guimet 61625 in the following date *fulgiyan tasha aniya, ninggun biyai ice de*, that is, 1st of the 6th month of the red-tiger-year, corresponding to 24th June 1626 (see Pang/Stary 1998, p. 45). Since this third propitious omen is missing in the xylograph, we may suppose that it was cut before that event could be included. The xylograph must therefore have been completed between 1623 and 1626.

The Manchu and the Chinese versions do not coincide in many cases: their contents shows additions or omissions, probably according to the Manchu or Chinese addressees and their different cultural backgrounds, as can often be seen in so-called "parallel" (*hebi* 合璧) poetical compositions.[18]

---

14 A biography of Dahai is found in *Hummel*, p. 213, and *Linke*, p. 112–120. For his role in the script reform see T. A. Pang, "The Manchu script reform of 1632: New data and new questions", in J. Janhunen & V. Rybatzki (eds.), *Writing in the Altaic World*, Helsinki 1999, pp. 201–206; M. Weiers, "Ein Blockdrucktext betreffend die orthographische Präzisierung der Buchstaben ohne Punkte und Kreise durch Dahai". *Zentralasiatische Studien* 29 (1999), pp. 87–96; M. Weiers, "Einige Bemerkungen zur Geschichte der Entwicklung der mandschurischen Schrift". *Acta Orientalia Academiae Scientiarum Hungaricae* 55/1–3 (2002), 269–279.
15 *Linke*, p. 230; for Kūrcan's biography see *Linke*, p. 124–133.
16 *Linke*, p. 222.
17 *Linke*, p. 114.
18 For examples, see G. Stary, "Linguistic and cultural limits of Manchu poetry in comparison with Chinese", in *Altai Hakpo/Journal of the Altaic Society of Korea* 17 (2007), pp. 85–92. For differences between the Manchu and Chinese versions found in the xylograph see T. A. Pan, "Obraščenie Pozdnej Czin' k dinastii Min", in *Pis'mennye pamjatniki Vostoka*, 7, Moskva 2007, pp. 5–20.

The Manchu and Chinese text

Adopted transliteration for old Manchu: ỹ = i>y, c̣ = j>c, s̄ = s>š, ō = o>ū, ś = s>z
For the punctuation of the Chinese text see Pan Zhe (1984)
δ = big *birga*, ○ = small *birga*

[Opening paragraph]

(Manchu)   (Chinese)

	(Manchu)	(Chinese)	
1 δ abka nai siran de niỹalma c̣i fusihōn umiỹaha ỹerhuwe ci uwasihun gemu abkai banjibuhangge abka ūjimbi kai:	In the space between Heaven and Earth, from men to insects, all are creatures of Heaven, and Heaven nourishes them.	In the space between Heaven and Earth, from mankind to insects, all [...] Heaven created and Heaven nourishes them.	**1** 天地之間上自人類下至昆虫趕[ ]天生天養之也
nikan sini banjibuhanggeo si ūjimbio:	Are they your creatures, oh Chinese, do you nourish them?	Does your Southern Dynasty create and nourish them?	是你南朝生之養之乎
wanli han-i mūjilen gōwaliỹabi: abka be daburakō: mini gūrun amban c̣ooha geren: ỹehe be wac̣i ūjic̣i mini c̣iha dana **2** seme: jasei tūlergi enc̣u gūrun-i ūile de *tanahangge**	Emperor Wanli had a change of heart, he did not defer to Heaven. Saying: "My Empire is great, the soldiers are numerous, to destroy or to nourish the Yehe depends on my will, respect it!", he committed a crime against a foreign country outside [his] borders.	Emperor Wanli's heart was not righteous, [...] [.........] without Earth; trusting to the Empire's great army, create [....] [........................] a foreign country outside [his] borders.	萬曆皇帝心不公[ ] [ ][ ]無地恃其國大兵眾生[ ] [ ][ ][ ][ ]邊外他國
mini mafa ama *de aika*** ūile bio	As for my grandfather and father, what crime did they commit?	As for my grandfather [........................] [........................]	將我祖[ ] [ ][ ][ ][ ] [ ]

---

* "tanahangge" substitues the cancelled "tabi".
** "de aika" substitutes the cancelled "be umai".

Opening paragraph

(akō babi waka:)*** jai ỹehe de dabi mini ỹabubi jafan būhe sargan be monggo de būhe:	(There is no guilt.) Later I helped the Yehe, [but their] woman who was promised [to me and] for whom I had [already] given bridal gifts, was given to a Mongol.	Later, helping Beiguan, I [....................] [........................] [........................]	又 助 北 關 將 我 [ ] [ ] [ ] [ ] [ ] [ ] [ ] [ ] [ ]
jai geli ỹehei niỹalmai gisun be gaibi mini sancara: fanaha: caiha: feideri: giỹaho sancin: ū elkeo: jang 3 baisi: ban cang ioi, jakōn gooi niỹalmai tehe boo be tuwa sindame: taribi ỹangsaha jeku be gaibuhakō bosioho.	Later, having accepted the words of the Yehe people, the houses of the people of my eight territories of Sancara, Fanaha, Caiha, Feideri, Giyahū Sancin, U Elkeo, Jang Baisi, Ban Cang Ioi were set on fire; after having cultivated and weeded [their fields], they could not gather in the grain and were expelled.	[....] accepted Beiguan [....] [....................] Feide[..], [..............], Wu Erkou, the Zhang clan [....................] [.............], houses of the people living [...] territories, all [........] were not allowed to gather in [the grain of] the fields, and all [....].	聽 北 關 **2a** [ ] [ ] [ ] [ ] [ ] [ ] [ ] [ ] 非 德 [ ] [ ] [ ] [ ] [ ] 吳 兒 口 張 其 哈 剌 [ ] [ ] [ ] [ ] 處 人 住 的 房 室 盡 行 [ ] [ ] [ ] 過 田 地 不 准 收 割 俱 各 皆 [ ]
waka ūilengge ỹehe be mūrime ūjiki: ūru niỹalma mimbe mūrime waki seme	[You] were determined to nourish the guilty and bad Yehe and determined to kill me, a righteous man.	Although the people of Beiguan are not righteous, [you] obstinately wanted to nourish [......], but wanted to kill me, a righteous man, at all costs.	且 以 北 關 不 正 之 人 強 欲 生 [ ] 我 本 公 正 之 人 必 欲 殺 之
jing gidašame minci hokorakō obi bi usabi wanli han-i arbun mimbe ainaha 4 seme ujirakō seme mini koroko kirihe ba be bithe arabi abka de hašabi dain deribuhe:	[Since you] often used violence and did not spare me, I lost hope [and became certain] that it was not in Emperor Wanli's nature ever to nourish me. After having put on paper my grief and	[Since you] often used violence, these circumstances became unbearable for me [and] it was impossible to be more patient; therefore I submitted to Heaven a memorial [describ-	屢 行 欺 逼 勢 不 容 我 含 忍 不 過 **2b** 故 將 我 歷 來 苦 辱 之 情 具 奏 上 天 方 敢 起 兵

*** "akō babi waka" is cancelled without substitution.

Opening paragraph

	sorrow, I announced these accusations to Heaven [and then] war broke out.	ing] all the former grief and sorrow; then I dared to send [my] army.	
eiten jaka be nei- gen ūjire abka ū- nenggi tondo obi:	Since Heaven, nour- ishing equally all beings, is honest and righteous,	Since Heaven nour- ishes all ten thou- sand beings, it is the most honest and with- out selfishness;	養 天 普 賴 實 萬 之 公 無 私 至
amba gūrun seme dere banirakō wa- ka be wakalaha: ajige gūrun seme gōniha akō ūru be ūrulehe:	not considering [how] great an empire could be, it considers injus- tice to be unjust, and not thinking [how] a kingdom could be small, it considers justice to be just.	not considering [the fact that] the South- ern Dynasty has the appearance of a great empire, [Heaven] pun- ished it for its injus- tice; not considering [the fact that] my [..] is a small kingdom, [Heaven] perceives [my] justice and sup- ports [me].	不 以 南 朝 為 大 國 容 情 而 仍 責 其 不 公 不 以 我 [ ] 小 國 仍 鑒 公 正 而 佑 之
niyalmai ciha oci amba gūrun-i cang- gi banjimbidere: 5 ajige gūrun bimbio:	According to man's opinion, only great empires should live; could small empires exist?	According to man's opinion, great em- pires [.......]; small empires should not exist.	若 依 人 心 論 [ ][ ] 大 國 而 無 有 小 國 也
ūnenggi tondo jur- gan-i ūile beidere de ūlin hono gaija- rakō kai:	If a case is judged in a fair manner, [even] a small property could not be extorted.	[..........] in a fair manner, no[body] extorts property.	但 從 公 道 [ ] [ ] [ ] 賄 賂 且 不 敢 受
nikan si yehei jūwe hoton-i beile yang- giyanu cinggiyanu be ūile beidembi seme: hecen-i duka de jalidame gamabi: umai ūile akō 6 ni- yalma be babi waha:	Oh Chinese, saying that you will judge the crimes of the Beile of the two Yehe cities, Yang- giyanu and Cinggi- yanu, you took the city gates by deceit and killed innocent people to no purpose.	Formerly [your] South- ern Dynasty [..........] [.....]jianu and Cheng- jianu, with the subter- fuge to judge their [...] [............................] [............................]	前 南 朝 將 [ ][ ][ ][ ] 迦 奴 逞 家 奴 推 說 斷 其 [ ][ ][ ] [ ][ ][ ][ ] [ ][ ]
abkai banjihuba emu gūrun-i ejen beise be babi wa-	To kill the *Beise* [or] rulers of a kingdom created by Heaven en	[.................] Heaven created a kingdom [...] [............................]	[ ][ ] 天 生 一 國 **3a** [ ] [ ][ ][ ][ ]

Opening paragraph

Manchu	Translation 1	Translation 2	Chinese
hangge: ter-e sūi abida genembi abka sinde isibumbi kai:	vain - where should such a crime lead? Heaven will pay you back for it.	Heaven will pay you back [for it].	天必報矣
nikan si onggoho sembidere: abka onggombio:	Oh Chinese, you probably forgot it! Will Heaven forget it?	Your Southern Dynasty [....] [...........] How [.......] Heaven forget?	你南朝[ ] [ ][ ][ ]蒼 天豈忘乎
7 ajige gūrun bimbio:	Will a small kingdom live?		
nikan si amba gūrun necin neigen-i banjici: sini dere be siyun-i gese: sini beye be alin-i gese:	When your great empire, oh Chinese, is living peacefully, your face will be like the sun; you yourself will be like a mountain;	When you are honest and unselfish, [......] your face will be like sunshine, you yourself will be like a high mountain;	爾若公平 無私[ ][ ] [ ]爾面如 日光身如 太山
sini mūjilen be mederi gese gōnime ūwe ai gelerakō ehe gōnici ombi:	your heart will be like an ocean; thinking [this],who could think badly [of you] without being afraid?	the heart will be like a wide [..] [..] could dare [to say that] there is even a tiny crime?	心如滄[ ] [ ]敢私毫 有犯
sini mūjilen gōwaliyabi ehe de niyalma ehe gōnici ombi kai:	After having a change of heart, [becoming] a man [involved] in bad things, [you now] have bad thoughts.	Since you had a change of heart, doing [.......] [.....] honestly, therefore [you committed] crimes.	因爾改變 初心行[ ] [ ]公以此 犯耳
jūlgeci ebsi emu halai 8 niyalma enteheme han-i akōmbuha kooli:	From ancient times there are always examples of men belonging to a certain family, who became Emperors.	From ancient times there was [always] somebody from a certain family who succeeded in becoming an Emperor.	自古以來 豈有一姓 之中嘗為 帝王
emu han-i beye minggan tumen se bahame banjiha kooli bio:	Is there any example of an Emperor who lived to reach the age of ten million years?	Did any ruler reach the age of ten million [years]?	一君身壽 延千萬
abka kemuni halame han tebuhebi kai:	It was always Heaven which, changing, appointed Emperors.	It was always Heaven which, changing, [made Emperors] succeed [or] fail.	乃天運循 還也
cin še hōwang han	Emperor Cin Ši	The Qin Emperor Lü	秦王呂政

Opening paragraph

enduringge jūlgei han be teburakō:	Hōwang was not enthroned as a divine Emperor of ancient times:	Zheng was not like an Emperor of ancient times:	不等古時帝王
ini beẏebe tuktan han sehebi:	He proclaimed himself the First Emperor.	He called himself First Supreme Emperor.	自稱為始皇帝
ini jui be jai jalan-i han sehebi:	His son was proclaimed Emperor of the Second Generation.	The son was called [Emperor of the] Second Generation.	子為二世
terei **9** dolo ini hōnc̣ihin be abka nai gese enteheme han-i akōmbumbi:	Inwardly [he was convinced that] his relatives would become eternal emperors, as Heaven and Earth, saying that he will be immortal and live for Eternity.	[He was convinced] he would rule for ten million [years], as Heaven and Earth.	以至千 **3b** 萬與天地同久
ini beẏe be būc̣ere akō enteheme banjimbi sehebi kai:			
gōniha jurgan fudasihōn: ẏabuha jurgan ehe obi abka wakalabi:	Since [his] thoughts took a wrong turn and [his] actions became bad, he committed a crime against Heaven.	Since his thoughts took a wrong turn, [he] infuriated the Supreme Heaven.	因其想念不正上天致怒
ama jui damu tofohon aniẏa han tebi doro efujehebi:	After father and son had ruled as Emperors for fifteen years, they lost their reign.	Father and son [ruled] fifteen years, then they lost Heaven's [........].	父子十五年而天 [ ]
wanli han abka be daburakō:	Emperor Wanli did not defer to Heaven.	Emperor Wanli did not defer to the Mandate of Heaven.	萬曆皇帝不由天命
ini beẏe be **10** abka arabi:	He considered himself to be the Heaven.		
ūilei ūru waka be bodorakō:	He did not distinguish right and wrong in things.	He did not distinguish right and wrong in things.	不論事之是非
waka niẏalma be ūjiki: ūru niẏalma be waki sehebe abka wakalabi wanli han-i ama jui siran	By nourishing unjust people and killing just people, he was disapproved of Heaven; therefore Emperor	Wishing to kill just people, and [..........] unjust people, he provoked Heaven's wrath; [........] a short period	是者反欲殺之非者反 [ ][ ] 之以致天怒不數年間

siran-i būcehe kai:	Wanli, father and son, perished one after another	[....] [.........] and perished.	[ ][ ][ ][ ] 而 亡
niyalma-i ciha oci: cin še hōwang-i ama jui: wanli han i ama jui ai de būcembi: abkai ciha obi tuttu kai:	According to human desires, how could Cin Ši Hūwang, father and son, and Wanli, father and son, die? It happened according to Heaven's desire!	According to human desires, Qin Huang [......................] because [...........] [........]	若 依 人 心 秦 皇 [ ][ ] [ ][ ][ ][ ] [ ][ ]以 [ ] [ ] 4a 也
11 jalan jalan-i kooli de ỹai-a han niyalma abka ci wasika: na ci tūcike kooli akō: inu niyalma de banjibubi: eture jeterengge baharakō beỹebe sūilabubi: jobolon gasacun de dosabume mūjilen be jobobubi: eiten jobolon be doosobubi han ohongge ambula kai:	In the books [handed down] from generation to generation, no man is recorded who came down from Heaven or came out from Earth as Emperor. Having been born as man without clothes and food, he had to make personal efforts, he had to suffer harm and sorrow, he had to harden his heart, and then, after having borne all kinds of harm, when he became an Emperor, he was a great one.	[..........................] generation to generation, an Emperor [...] in general from [.....] from Earth a man's [.............] without clothes and food, he had to suffer harm and sorrow; after having borne all kinds of harm, when he became an Emperor, then [............].	[ ][ ][ ][ ] [ ][ ] 歷 代 帝 王 [ ] 有 從 [ ][ ][ ] 從 地 生 出 大 抵 是 人 之 [ ][ ] 使 之 無 衣 無 食 受 苦 受 難 險 阻 備 嘗 而 後 為 天 子 者 往 [ ][ ] 之

Comment

Nurhaci's introduction to his "proclamation" opens with a "big *birga*" [𜷀][1] and refers to the well-known concept of "Heaven's Justice" which – as will be discussed later with detailed examples – causes the bestowal or revocation of a dynasty's

---

1　The beginning of the following examples are all marked with a "small *birga*", i. e. a *circellus* (O). On the *birga* see M. Weiers, pp. 276–277 in his article "Zur Registratur der mandschurischen Holztäfelchen über Ajiges Invasion der Ming im Jahre 1636", in M. Gimm, G. Stary, M. Weiers (eds.), *Aetas Manjurica* 6, Wiesbaden 1998, pp. 251–314.

"Heavenly Mandate" *tianming* 天命. The Ming emperors appear therefore from the very beginning as unworthy rulers, in opposition to Nurhaci whose "just" actions are represented as approved by Heaven. This situation is concretely described by quoting the Ming dynasty's support of the Yehe tribe, the murder (1582) of Nurhaci's father Giocangga and grandfather Taksi, the "illegitimate" marriage of a Yehe woman, promised to Nurhaci, to the Mongol prince Manggultai, the son of Darhan of the Kalka Mongols, the Ming army's intrusion into the territory claimed by Nurhaci and the consequent distruction of his subjects' harvest. All these accusations were part of the famous so-called "seven grievances",[2] which Nurhaci announced to Heaven on 7th May 1618 to justify his war against the Ming. He also adds, as a proof of the Ming's outrageous behaviour against Heaven, the murder of the two Yehe leaders Yanggiyanu and Cinggiyanu in 1584.[3] After these events, Nurhaci then compares the destiny of Qin Shih huangdi 秦始皇帝 and his son, Hu Hai 胡亥, (Ershi huangdi 兒世皇帝), who together ruled for 15 years (221–207 BC), with that of the Ming Emperors Zhu Yijun 朱翊鈞 (Wanli 萬曆) and his son Zhu Changluo 朱常洛 (Taichang 泰昌),[4] who, like Qin Shi huangdi's son, died soon after having ascended the throne. The mention of the Taichang emperor is an important clue to dating the "proclamation": since he died on 26th September, 1620, it must have been compiled after that date. A comparison of the two texts is illuminating because it provides the first instance of a difference in Manchu and Chinese historical nomenclature: referring to the "First Emperor", the Chinese text gives his name "Lü Zheng" 呂政,[5] while the Manchu text quotes the evidently better known usual title C̱in še hōwang han (= Cin Ši hūwang han), i.e. Qin Shi huangdi. We also note, from the very beginning, the different appellation used for the Ming dynasty: for the Chinese reader, the less offensive form "ni nanchao 你南朝 – your southern dynasty", is used, which is substituted in the Manchu text with a less respectful "nikan – [you] Chinese". Noteworthy also are stylistic differences, found, for example in the Manchu text f. 9, and the corresponding Chinese text f. 3b: 千萬 (*qianwan* = 1.000x10.000) is given in Manchu with a simple *enteheme* ("eternally"), and the following Manchu sentence *ini beẏe be bucere akō enteheme banjimbi sehebi kai* ("...saying that he will be immortal and live for eternity") is missing, as not seldomly happens, in the Chinese version.

---

2   The presumably original text of these "seven grievances" is found in *JMZD*, I, pp. 181-189; for an analysis and the historical background see G. Stary, "La politica mancese delle sette accuse: Una costante per giustificare la conquista della Cina e della Corea", in G. Bellingeri and G. Vercellin (eds.), *Studi in onore di Mario Grignaschi*, Venezia 1988, pp. 43-55 (Eurasiatica 5: Quaderni del Dipartimento di Studi Eurasiatici, Università di Venezia).
3   See *Hummel*, pp. 897–898, under Yangginu.
4   See *Hummel*, pp. 176–177.
5   See *Chavannes*, II, p. 100.

[1st example]

12 ○ bi donjici: jūlge nikan gūrun-i siyŏn gebungge niyalmai banjiha eme ajigan de akō obi: ama gūseo mentuhun farhōn. banirke eme: banirke eme de banjiha jui hiyang ni gisun de dosibi: siyŏn be waki seme amai yadara hūcin fete seme dosimbubi hūcin-i angga de uwehe gidahabi:

I heard that in the ancient Chinese Empire a man called Šūn was born, whose mother died when he was small. [His] father Guseo was stupid and ignorant. He agreed with the words of the stepmother and of the stepmother's son, Hiyang, who wanted to kill Šūn. Ordering him to dig a well demanded by [his] father, they ordered him to go in and covered the well's opening with a stone.

[I] heard that Shun's father was ignorant; he listened to the words of the stepmother and Xiang, who wished to kill Shun. They ordered him to dig a well, and then they closed it.

頑父母嘗使舜後之言欲殺舜浚井而掩之象

13 abka siyŏn-i tondo sain be tuwabi hūcin ci tūcibuhebi:

When Heaven saw Šūn's uprightness and goodness, it let him get out from the well.

Heaven showed him mercy [because] he was upright and let him get out from a side way.

天孝之 **4b** 憫其出從旁

siyŏn yadahōn obi beye ūsin ūileme* banjihabi:

Since Šūn was poor, he lived working in the fields.

Since he was poor and destitute, he cultivated the fields at Lishan all on his own.

因乃窮躬歷山不耕遇于

amala abkai erin isinjibi han ohobi.

Later, when the time [established] by Heaven had come, he became an Emperor.

Later Heaven's Mandate was handed down to him, and he got an Empire.

後之天下命遂歸有天

abka emhun fūsihōn be tuwarakō tondo erdemu be tuwame ūwehiyeme ūwasimbuhe

Heaven favours or overthrows having no regard [if a man is] alone or poor, but taking account

Heaven does not consider [if a man is] poor or alone; it only takes into account his virtues, and, silently pro-

天貧惟默此不賤論祐其論其孤其德爲帝一也

---

* ūileme ("working") substitutes the cancelled tarime ("cultivating").

1st example

kooli ere emu:	of [his] righteousness and virtues. This is the first example of the rise and fall [of a dynasty].	tecting him, makes him an Emperor. This is the first [example].	
ere kooli be tuwaci niyalmai **14** gōnihangge tašan: abkai gōnihangge ūnenggi kai: ama guseoi gōnihai oci siyŏn-i ergen bimbio. abkai gōnihai obi siyŏn be han obuha bikai: nikan si entehe be gōnirakō: abka be daburakō sini gūrun amban cooha geren seme šerici abka geli simbe sini ciha obumbio:	When reading this example, [it is seen that] the man's thoughts are illusions, Heaven's thoughts are reality. According to father Guseo's design, could there be a life for Šūn? [But] according to Heaven's design, Šūn was made an Emperor. Oh Chinese, didn't you think about this? If you, not considering Heaven, oppress [people] and threaten [me with] your troops saying that they are numerous and your empire is great, how could Heaven follow you in your desires!	It can be seen that [everything] depends on Heaven and [...] on men. According to Gusou's design, Shun [.......] [.....] able to nourish; moreover, was not there an Empire too? [........................] know this story which does not correspond to the will of Heaven. [..] [........................] numerous, blustering and oppress people, how can Heaven follow you in this! [........................]	可 見 由 天 由 [ ] 人 矣 若 依 瞽 瞍 之 心 舜 [ ] [ ] [ ] [ ] 能 保 況 有 天 下 乎 [ ] [ ] [ ] [ ] 鑒 古 事 不 順 天 意 [ ] **5a** [ ] [ ] [ ] [ ] 多 大 言 欺 人 天 豈 遂 爾 之 [ ] [ ] [ ] [ ]

Comment

The first episode recounts the well-known life and destiny of the mythical emperor Shun 舜 (2317–2208). The parallel with Nurhaci is evident: both were of humble origin, but both were supported by Heaven thanks to their loyal and upright behaviour. Shun's "stupid and ignorant" (*mentuhn farhūn*) father Guseo (Gusou 瞽瞍, who is not mentioned in the Chinese text) is compared here with the Ming emperor; the Manchu text is also the only one which specifies that "Siyang" (Xiang 象) was the stepbrother of Shun (*banirke eme de banjiha jui*: "a child born of the stepmother") – an explanation which evidently was not needed for the more educated Chinese readers who were supposed to know the story reported in Sima Qian's 司馬遷 *Shij* 史記. (See *Chavannes*, I, 71–76). The episode is not found neither in the *Shi-*

lu, the *JMZD*, the *KKFL*, nor in Nurhaci's "Teachings" *Enduringge Tacihiyan / Shengxun* 聖訓,[1] but is briefly mentioned in Guimet mss. 61624 (p. 48) and 61625 (p. 92–93), where we read: [92] *Genggiỹen han hendume: bi donjici jūlge nikan gūrun i siỹun gebungge niỹalma ūsin ūileme banjiha bi: banjiha eme ajihan de būcebi: ama gūseo : banireke emei gisun de dosibi: siỹun be hocin de gidame wahabi: abkai cohome fulinggai banjibuha niỹalma obi* [93] *abka dalibi būcebuheko hocin ci tūcibubi amala abkai erin isinjibi han oho sere:* "The Illuminated Khan spoke: 'I heard that in the ancient Chinese empire a man named Siỹun was living, working in the fields. His natural mother died when he was small. His father Gūseo agreed with the stepmother's exhortation to kill him by throwing him into a well. [But] since he was a man having Heaven's special fortune, Heaven protected him and he came out from the well and did not die. When later the moment [determined] by Heaven came, he became an emperor'."

---

[1] For Nurhaci's "Teachings" see G. Stary, "Some Preliminary Remarks on the Authenticity and Historical Value of Qing Taizu Nurhaci's 'Holy Teachings' – The Manchu Version ('Enduringge Tacihiyan')", in *Central Asiatic Journal* 49/1 (2005), pp. 60-70

[2nd example]

15 ○ jai geli donjici: jeo gūrun-i hiowan wang han-i fonde han-i hecen -i buẙa jūse: amba asigan gemu siẙōn ẙamjime falanggō dūme ūculeme biẙa teni mūkdembi: siẙōn teni tūhembi: nimalan moo ji orho: jeo gūrun be efulembi:	Furthermore, [I] also heard: In the time of king Hiowan of the Jeo dynasty, when the sun approached the evening, all children – old and young – of the Emperor's city clapped their hands and sang: "The moon will rise, the sun will set, the mulberry tree and the *Ji* grass will destroy the Jeo dynasty."	Furthermore [I] heard: In the time of king Xuan [....], the people in the city sang: "The moon is rising, the sun is setting, the mulberry tree and the *Ji* grass will surely destroy the Zhou dynasty".	又聞 [ ] 宣 王時市中 有民謠云 月將升日 將沒檿弧 箕服實亡 周國
tuttu ūculerebe hecen gidarara coohai niẙalma donjibi bithe arabi han de alara **16** jaka de han šasulabi hendume	When the soldiers who oppressed the city heard these songs, they wrote a letter and made a report to the Emperor who, being confused, asked:	When Emperor Xuan heard it, he became very afraid and asked:	宣王聞之 大驚問曰
ere gisun ai serengge: sioomu gebungge amban hendume:	"What do these words mean?" A dignitary named Sioomu [fore-]told:	"Does this song indicate fortune or misfortune?" The great dignitary Shao Mu explained to the Throne:	此謠主何 吉凶大臣 召穆奏曰
nimalan moo be beri arambi: ji orho be ladu arambi: mini mentuhun-i dolo gūrun de amala beri sirdan-i jobolon bi sembi:	"Making bows from mulberry trees and making quivers from *Ji* grass means, according to my humble opinion, that bows and arrows will later provoke trouble in the country."	"Mulberry trees and *Ji* grass reveal that the country will suffer misfortune from bows and arrows."	檿弧箕服 主國有弓 矢之禍
han hendume tuttu oci hecen-i dorgi beri sirdan	The Emperor said: "If it is so, then all the producers of	Emperor Xuan said: "What would happen if all the producers of	宣王曰 **5b** 盡殺造 弓矢之人

arara niyalma be gemu wara: kūi beri 17 sirdan be gemu tuwa sindara oci antaka:	bows and arrows inside the city should be killed. What would happen if all the bows and arrows in the depositories are set on fire?"	bows and arrows were killed, and the depositories where the the bows and arrows are kept, are burnt?"	燒藏弓矢之庫何如
tede beyang fu gebungge amban hendume bi abkai arbun be tuwaci : tere ganio han-i hōwai dolo bi:	Then the dignitary named Beyang Fu said: "Looking at Heaven's appearrance, [I see that] this omen refers to inside the court.	The Grand Astrologer Boyang Fu said: "I look at Heaven's appearance [and I see that] misfortune is inside the palace.	太史令伯陽父曰臣觀天象禍在宮中
beri sirdan-i ūile waka: amaga jalan de urunakō hehe ejen tūcibi gūrun be facuhōrambi:	It is not a matter of bows and arrows. In a later generation surely a female ruler will appear and contest the empire.	It is not a matter of bows and arrows.	非干弓矢之事
tere anggala biya teni mukdembi: siyōn teni tūhembi sehebi 18 siyōn serengge han niyalmai arbun: tūhembi serengge sain akō: biya serengge hehe niyalmai arbun mukdembi serengge hehe ejen tūcibi doro be facuhōrarangge yargiyan kai:	The real [meaning] of somebody's: 'The moon will rise, the sun will set', is [the following]: 'sun' refers to the ruler's person, 'will set' refers to [his] misfortune, 'moon' refers to a female person, 'will rise' means that a female ruler will rise and contend the rule".	[In] the song 'The moon will rise, the sun will set', [the word] 'sun' refers to the ruler's [..], 'will set' refers to an unlucky omen, 'moon' refers to an Empress's [..], [..] means that a female ruler will contend the Empire."	況謠曰月將升日將沒日者人君之[ ]沒者不祥之兆月者后妃之[ ][ ]者當以亂天下
han ūile akō irgen be wara: coohai agōra be tuwa sindara oci ombio seme tafulame nakabuha: tereci hio-	How can an Emperor kill innocent people and set the army's weapons on fire! With these words of warning he restrained	[....................] kill innocent people, and burn the [.......] with bows and arrows! [..............] then the Emperor died, and the	[ ][ ][ ]殺無罪之人燒弓矢之 6a [ ][ ][ ]后王崩子幽王立

2nd example

wan wang han **19** bederehe manggi: jui Io wang sirame han tebi: boose nioi gebungge fūjin-i gisun de dosibi fūjin etenggi lebi doro efujehe sere: abkai joriha ganio jurcehekō efujehe kooli ere jūwe:	[the Emperor]. Then Hiowan Wang died, and his son Io Wang ascended the Throne. He agreed with the words of [his] consort named Boose Nioi; when the consort used [all her] power, the rule was lost. Not to change [when] an omen is shown by Heaven, will lead to ruin. This is the second example.	son Yu Wang ascended the Throne. He agreed with the words [.....], [.....] the empire was destroyed. Not recognize Heaven's omen will finally [...] ruin. This is the second [example].	聽 言 [ ] [ ] [ ] [ ] 以 亡 天 下 天 兆 不 違 終 [ ] 敗 亡 此 其 二 也
ere kooli be nikan si sarhōn:	This example, oh Chinese, didn't you know it?		
fūsi be gaiha suwaẙan morin aniẙa: nikan-i namgin-i hecen de tūcike jūlgei **20** uwehe de araha bithe de: siẙōn siẙōn waka ombi: biẙa biẙa waka ombi serengge sini amba genggiẙen akō ojorongge wakao: abkai jorihangge gūwembio: atanggi bicibe isimbi kai:	When Fusi was taken in the year of the yellow horse, on an ancient stone unearthed in the city of Nanjing this inscription was engraved: "A moon is not the moon, a sun is not the sun." Your Great Light is not immortal! How to avoid what is indicated by Heaven – whenever it will be it will happen!	In the year of the conquest of Fushun, a stone with this inscription was discovered in your [city of] Nanjing: "A moon is not the moon, a sun is not the sun." If this is not an omen of the Great Light's [~ Da Ming] fall! This is Heaven's will, how can men oppose it!	克 撫 順 之 年 爾 南 京 出 一 石 碑 有 云 陰 不 陰 陽 不 陽 豈 非 大 明 將 亡 之 兆 也, 天 意 如 此 人 豈 能 違 乎

Comment

The second "example" quotes two interpretations of a popular song referring to the Zhou dynasty's king Xuan Wang 宣 王 (827–782 BC) and his son Yu Wang 幽 王 (r. 781–772 BC), who perished with his consort Bao Si 褒 姒 because of her unworthy behaviour.¹ The parallel between the two dynasties Zhou and Ming is provided by the misinterpretation and disregard of a premonitory omen sent by Heaven: the Zhou dynasty's song on the "moon and sun" is compared with a similar text found on a stone-inscription unearthed in Nanjing in 1618, the year Nurhaci conquered Fushun. This omen on the stone in Nanjing had also to be regarded as a serious warning from Heaven to the Ming emperor. As he did not take it seriously, according to Nurhaci's words, he would as a consequence suffer the same fate as the Zhou emperor.

Note that in the Chinese text the name of the astrologer Bo-yang Fu is given with the characters 伯 昜 父, in contrast with those given in the *Shiji*, i.e. 伯 陽 甫.² This difference could be considered as proof that the erudite compiler(s) of the Chinese text knew the episode, but did not copy it directly from the *Shiji*; rather their sources are based on popular novels as seen from the episode on Zhu Yuanzhang.³ Last but not least, it should be noted that *Namgin* – the old Manchu writing – is used for Nanjing and that in the last sentence the Manchu wordplay "Great Light" (*Amba Genggiyen*) is used for "Da Ming" (Great Ming [Dynasty]).

---

1 See *Chavannes*, I, pp. 283–284: "Au temps du roi *Siuen*, une petite fille chanta, disant: 'Celui qui a un arc fait avec du bois de mûrier sauvage et un carquois fait de roseaux, celui-là certainement perdra le royaume dés Tcheou'. [...] La fille [...] vint du pays de Pao et c'est purquoi on l'appela Pao-se. [...] Pao-se fut faite reine et [...] le grand astrologue Po-yang dit: 'Le malheur est consommé; il n'y a plus moyen d'y échapper'". Pao Si became a famous figure in Chinese literature, especially in the *Dong Zhou Lieguo zhi* 東周列國志 compiled in Ming times, and has also been studied by H. Kopsch in his article "Pao-sze. The Cleopatra of China" (*China Review* IV, 1875/76) and others: see *O. Franke*, III, p. 100.
2 See *Chavannes*, I, pp. 278–279.
3 See the "14th example".

[3rd example]

O geli donjici: cin še hōwang han amargi jase bitume y̌aburede: lūšeng gebungge niy̌alma 21 mederi de genebi amasi jibi: mederi ci bahabi gajiha tūsio bithe de:	Furthermore [I] heard: When Emperor Cin Ši Hūwang travelled to the northern border, a man named Lušeng went to sea; when he came back, he brought from the sea the book Tušu which he submitted to the Throne and in which is written:	Furthermore [I] heard: When Qin Shi Huang travelled to the northern border, Lusheng went to sea; when he came back, he submitted to the Throne the book *Lutu* in which is written:	又聞秦始 皇巡北邊 盧生入海 **6b** 還因奏 錄圖書曰
cin gūrun be hō efulembi seme arahabi seme hoolame arabi alibure jaka de: cin še hōwang han hendume hō serengge jasei tūlergi gūrun kai:	"Hū will destroy the Cin Empire." Emperor Cin Ši Hūwang said: "Hū is a state outside the border.	"Who will destroy Qin is Hu". Shi Huang said: "Hu is a state outside the border."	亡秦者胡 也始皇曰 胡乃邊外 之國也
jasei tūlergi gūrun mūse be efulembi seci jūwe siden be dalime hecen sahaki seme: 22 lin doo ba ci: lioodung ni ba de isitala tūmen ba funceme golmin hecen sahakabi: amala jasei tūlergi gūrun umainahakōbi:	If a state outside the border wishes to destroy us, we will construct a wall to divide both sides." From the territory of Lin Doo to Lioodung a wall more than ten thousand miles was built, and later the state outside the border did not provoke troubles.	Then a ten thousand miles long wall was built to avoid Hu. [But] later Hu did not provoke troubles.	遂筑長城 萬里以避 胡後胡無 事
ini jui hō hai sirame han tebi: doro akō ehe obi doro efulehe sere:	His son Hū Hai succeeded as Emperor; he was without *Dao* and bad, and [therefore] he lost the reign.	His son Hu Hai was without *Dao*, and therefore he lost the Empire.	其子胡亥 無道遂失 天下
abkai joriha ganio jurcerakō efulehe kooli ere ilan	Not recognizing an omen shown by Heaven will lead to ruin. This is the	Not recognizing an omen shown by Heaven, will finally lead to ruin. This is	天兆不違 終必敗亡 此其三也

3rd example

ere kooli be nikan si sarhōn:	third example. This example, oh Chinese, didn't you know it?	the third [example].	推背圖云
tūibei **23** tu bithe de jugiỹai han be sirarangge emu niỹalma beri jafabi ilihabi serengge:	In the book *Tūibei tu* is said: "A man, after having taken a bow and having founded [a dynasty], will succeed the Emperor of the Ju family".	The *Tuibei tu* says: "A [............] bow, founded [a dynasty]".	一 [ ][ ] 弓 立
aca̱bume ara̱ci jūšen sere hergen wakao: embi̱ci simbe ỹamaka jūšen gūrun dosibi efulembi: akō̱ci sini dorgi̱ci jūšen gebungge niỹalma tū̱cibi sini dorobe efulembi:	A Jušen script did not exist when this [book] was written! Was there any Jušen who entered [your] Empire to deposing you? If not – was there anyone called a Jušen, who was coming from inside your [Empire] to ruin your reign?	A Yi script did not exist, didn't it? Nobody knows about a man of the Yi who entered and ruled in the Middle Kingdom, or is there anyone in the Middle Kigdom with a Yi surname who caused trouble in the Empire?	豈非夷字耶 不知或夷人入主中國或中國 **7a** 別有夷姓名者以名者以亂天下也
abkai doigon de jorihangge gūwembio: atanggi **24** bi̱cibe isimbi kai:	How avoid what is indicated by Heaven beforehand – whenever it will be, it will happen.	Heaven showed an omen beforehand, [........] realized, finally cannot be avoided.	天預示兆 [ ][ ] 有驗 終不能違矣

Comment

This example is again devoted to the consequences of disregarding of Heaven's admonishing omens. The first part is devoted to Qin Shi huangdi and his unworthy son Hu Hai, and is based on the different interpretation of the character *hu* 胡: it refers to the "Eastern Barbarians", but is also the first component of Qin Shi huangdi's son's name. From the book of prophecies called *Lutu shu* 錄圖書,[1] found by

---

1 See the definition in *Cihai* 辭海 (Hongkong 1974), p. 1383, quoting the *Tongjian, Qin ji*, 32nd year of Qin Shi huangdi: *ru houshi chanwei zhi shu* 如後世讖緯之書 "a book for later generations to interprete prophecies."

the alchemist Lu Sheng 盧生 (see Chavannes, II, 167: "Maître Lo"),[2] the emperor knew that "Hu" would destroy his empire, and referred this term to the "Northern Barbarians", a reason for which he constructed the Great Wall (the geographic dimension of which – "from the territory of Lin Doo to Liyoodung" – is specified only in the Manchu text). The correct interpretation, however, connected "Hu" with his own son and was an admonishment from Heaven, which the emperor did not realize. As a consequence, and as already explained in the "Introduction" the dynasty came to an end.

The second part of this example is based on a prophecy found in the famous *Tuibei tu*,[3] where a "man with a bow" is told to bring about the fall of the "dynasty of the Zhu family" – this is, the Ming dynasty. According to Nurhaci's interpretation this man could only be he himself, since never before him had a "jušen" (= Jurchen, 女真 Nüzhen) successfully menaced the Ming empire. Again the Ming did not understand this prophecy, and their fate should therefore be considered as determined. Noteworthy, from a textual point of view is the puzzling Manchu *Tusio* (i.e. the old orthography for *Tušu*) *bithe* for the book *Lutu shu*: evidently the Manchu compiler did not understand in detail the Chinese term. Interesting is also the fact that, speaking about the "barbarians", the Chinese text uses the sometimes derogatory term Yi 夷, which in the Manchu version is substituted with the ethnonym "jušen".

---

2   See *Chavannes*, II, p. 167: "Maître *Lou*, originaire de *Yen*, avait été envoyé sur mer; à son retour, il prétexta quelque affaire des mânes et des dieux et en profita pour présenter un livre de *Lou-t'ou* où il était dit: «Ce qui perdra *Ts'in*, c'est *Hou*.» Alors *Che-hoang* envoya le général *Mong T'ien*, à la tête de trois cent mille soldats, attaquer les *Hou* sur la frontière du nord...".

3   Written by Li Chunfeng 李淳風 and Yuan Tiangang 袁天綱 during the times of Tang emperor Zhenguan 貞觀 (Tang Taizong, 627–649): see *Cihai*, p. 582.

[4th example]

○ geli donjici: liobang gebungge niyalma da de: cin han-i harangga emu gašan bosiokō bihebi:	Furthermore [I] heard: A man named Liobang was originally the head of a village belonging to the Cin Emperor.	Furthermore [I] heard: Liu Bang was originally a neighborhood head of Sishang; since the Qin [emperor] was without *Dao*, he created an army with simple people.	又聞劉邦 初為泗上 亭長見秦 無道以布 衣起兵
amala abkai erin isinjibi han ohobi:	Later, when the time determined by Heaven had come, he became an Emperor.	Later he got Heaven's Mandate, and established the Imperial lineage.	後天命有 歸而成帝 業
emhun fūsihōn be be tuwarakō: tondo erdemu be tuwame abkai ūwehiyeme ūwasimbuhe kooli ere duin:	[Heaven] favours or overthrows ignoring [if a man is] alone or poor, but considering [his] righteousness and virtues. This is the fourth example.	Heaven does not consider [if a man is] poor or alone; it only considers his virtues, and, silently protecting him, makes him an Emperor. This is the fourth [example].	天不論其 貧賤孤獨 惟論其德 默祐為帝 此其四也
amba gūrun 25 ajige gūrun-i haran: geren komsoi haran oci cin han-i doro ai de efujembi; lio bang ai de bahabi han tembi: abkai ciha serengge dere kai:	The fact that a country is great or small, and the fact that there are many or few [has no importance: the reason] why the rule of the Cin Emperor was lost, why it passed over to Lio Bang who became an Emperor, this is only the will of Heaven.	What concerns [the fact that] a country is great or small, or the circumstance of many or few [people, is of no importance]: how [it happened that] Qin lost and Liu Bang got an Empire - all these events are surely the intention of Heaven.	若論國之 大小勢之 眾寡秦 **7b** 何以失劉 邦何以得 天下凡事 必在天意 者此也
nikan si liyeliyebi dube be gōnirakō sini gūruni joborongge dere kai:	Oh Chinese, after becoming faint, you do not think about the end; [so] your Empire will go to ruin.	Your Southern Dynasty is faint, [but] your wisdom does not perceive it; therefore the country will go to ruin.	爾南朝昏 迷智不及 此所以國 家受禍也

Comment

This example refers to the well-known historical figure Liu Bang 劉邦 (247–195 BC), the founder of the Han dynasty, whose life and destiny is compared with that of Nurhaci. Both, being of humble origins, enjoyed Heaven's support because of their "righteousness and virtues". We note that in the Chinese text Liu Bang is called *tingzhang* ("neighborhood head"),[1] a title which in the Manchu text is simply given as bosiokō (> bošoku), "corporal" (*lingcui* 領催) in Qing times, and that he created an army against the Qin emperor who was "without Dao – *wu dao* 無道": there is no information about or reference whatsoever to Sishang are missing in the Manchu text, giving the impression that such detailed facts from ancient Chinese history could not interest the Manchu reader. Liu Bang is also briefly mentioned in the *JMZD* (V, 2041), where Nurhaci says that "...Heaven too loved him and made him the king of the Han [dynasty]..." (*tere be inu abka gosibi han wang han obi...*).

---

1 See *Hucker* n. 6750.

[5th example]

○ geli donjici: nikan-i han gūrun-i s'oos'oo **26** gebungge amban: tanggō tūmen cooha gaibi ū gūrun de genebi gūrun-i dūbe de cooha ilibi daha seme šerime takōrara jaka de: ū gūruni ejen sūn ciowan bithei mergese doroi ambasa be isabubi daharao eljereo seme hebedere de: bithei mergese doroi ambasa hendume:

s'oos'oo-i cooha **27** tanggō tūmen: mūsei cooha ilan tūmen afaci hūsun isirakō: dahaci jūse sargan ci fakcarakō: cooha bucere akō: gūrun sūilarakō: dahaci sain seme henduhe manggi: jai geli coohai buya niyalmai baru hebedere jaka de: coohai buya niyalma hendume: bithei mergese doroi ambasa gemu cini **28** beye ceni

Furthermore [I] heard: The dignitary Z'ooz'oo of the Chinese Han dynasty took one million soldiers, went to the State of U and drew up the soldiers on the State's border; after having sent a message with the order to surrender, the ruler of the State of U, Sūn Ciowan, assembled the ciil officials and the court dignitaries; during the discussion about whether to surrender or to resist, the civil officials and the court dignitaries said: "When Z'ooz'oo's one million soldiers fight against our thirty thousand soldiers, [our] forces will not be enough. If we surrender, we will not be separated from [our] children and wives, [our] soldiers will not die, the country will not suffer. It will be better if we surrender." After these words they also consulted the common soldiers, but the common soldiers said: "The civil officials and court digni-

Furthermore [I] heard: Cao Cao led one million soldiers to conquer Wu. When the great army had crossed the border, he sent a message to Wu with the order to come and to surrender. The ruler of Wu, Sun Quan, [...] [...] with all dignitaries; the civil officals said:

"Cao has one million of soldiers, we have [Our] forces which will not [be able to] resist. The best would be to surrender quickly, in order to save all [our] lives."
The military dignitaries said: "The civil dignitaries [.........] of all their wives and children, but not of the state.

又聞曹操
領兵百萬
伐吳大兵
壓境遣書
于吳令其
來降吳主
孫權[ ][ ]
于群臣時
文臣進日

曹兵百萬
我兵三萬
勢必不敵
8a 不如早
降保全生
靈

武臣進日
文臣[ ][ ]
皆各為妻
子不為國
家

5th example

jūse sargan-i banjire jalin de hendumbi: dahaci jūšen be kemuni jūšen amban be kemuni amban obumbi kai: gūrun-i ejen be gamabi wasimbure wara dabala ai obumbi niyalma bucere akō enteheme banjimbio: geren komsoi haran waka: abkai haran kai: afaki dere seme hendure jaka de: **29** coohai buya niyalmai gisun be ūrušebi: ashaha loho be tūcibubi tehe besergen be sacibi: jai jaka dahaki seme gisurehe manggi: ere besergen-i adali sacimbi seme hendubi:	taries speak all about their own and their childrens' and wives' lives. If we surrender, the people will remain people, the dignitaries will remain dignitaries. [But] when the country's ruler is captured, he will be deposed and killed: What will happen? Will people who are not killed live forever? What mathers is not which army is greater or smaller, but what Heaven decides what should happen. So we had better fight." When the words of the common soldiers were approved, [the emperor] took out his sword, cut into pieces the bed, and said that he would cut into pieces like that bed anybody who surrendered.	If we surrender, the dignitaries will automatically remain dignitaries, the people will automatically remain people. But in which country will the ruler be removed? Will the law of death not be valid for not old aged people? If [our] two armies fight against each other, inly Heaven will [decide] and not the greater or smaller number [of soldiers] which today will not have influence on the death-struggle." The king Wu agreed, took out his sword, cut into pieces the bed and said: "If any man dares to surrender, [I will cut him into pieces] like this bed."

降官民上且長之軍在在日之戰之砍人者同
投為為主地有兩只在今與死然刀降此案
若一自自置何未況戰意寡如一王拔日言
官民將於人生理交天眾不決吳乃案敢與

ilan tūmen coohai tanggō tūmen cooha be afabi etebi: sūn ciowan ū wang han-i gebu gaibi banjiha sere:	After thirty thousand soldiers had defeated one million soldiers in the battle, Sūn Ciowan reigned, accepting the title of of Emperor of U.	When these thirty thousand soldiers and Cao's one million fought against each other, [the latter] were defeated. After that [the winner] successfully conquered Jiangdong and completed [his] rule founding an Empire.

三曹相之江東鼎足之業
於是以與兵百萬大敗雄據成

abka geren **30** komso be tuwahakō ūru waka	Heaven does not consider [if a number is] great or small, but on-	Heaven does not consider [if the soldiers of an army are] nume-

勢只是
天不論
之眾寡
論事之

5th example

Manchu	English	English (cont.)	Chinese
be tuwame tondoi beidehe kooli ere sunja:	ly what is right and what is wrong and judges fairly. This is the fifth [example].	rous or few: it considers only what is right and what is wrong and judges fairly. This is the fifth [example].	非公斷此 其五也
nikan si ūru waka be bodorakō:	Oh Chinese, you do not distinguish right from wrong.	Your Southern Dynasty does not [......] right and wrong.	爾南朝不 [ ][ ]之是
gūrun amban cooha geren seme mūrime gōnirede: abka simbe wakalarangge dere kai:	Since you obstinately think only about the size of [your] Empire's great army, Heaven will blame you.	You believe only in the quantity of [your] Empire's great army, behaving obstinately and acting wrongfully; this provokes the Heaven's reproach.	非只恃國 大兵眾逆 理謬行以 致天怪也

Comment

With this example Nurhaci express the conviction that even a small army could win against a powerful enemy if Heaven's support is on its side. To prove the correctness of his words, he quotes the rivalry between Cao Cao 曹操 († 220 AD) and the king of Wu 吳, Sun Quan 孫權 († 251), who in 208 AD won a victory over his enemy in the battle of Chibi 赤壁, and in 229 AD became emperor of the Wu 吳 dynasty.[1] Certain passages of both texts are formulated according to whom they were addressed: the Manchu text only specifies that Cao Cao belonged to the "Chinese Han dynasty", and the Chinese text only adds that Sun Quan conquered Jiangdong before becoming Emperor.

---

1   For details see *O. Franke*, I, pp. 426–427.

[6th example]

○ jai meni gūrun-i kooli be tuwaci jūlge manju gūrun de aisin han tebi: jūšen 31 gūrun be gemu dahabubi banjihabi: tuttu banjirebe elerakō:

fūcihi bucerakō enteheme banjimbi sere fūcihi be baime genembi seme mujakū erin de giyang-i bira jūhe jafahabio tuwana seme jūwe jergi niyalma takōrabi: jūhe jafahakōbi seme alanjire jaka de gemu wahabi: ilaci jergi tuwana 32 seme takōraha niyalma: jūhe jafahakōbi seme alanaci wambi: jafahabi seme alanaci jafakōbi: adarame būcere seme songgoro de mūduri han tūcibi niyalmai beye ubaliyabi foncibi sūwe eitereci būcerengge: jūhe jafaha-

Furthermore [I] read in the book of our Dynasty: In the ancient Manchu state a [certain] Aisin Khan was on the Throne; he had subjugated the whole Ju£en country and ruled [over it]. Nevertheless, he was not satisfied with [his] life.

There was a Buddha who was said to be immortal and to live in eternity; [So the emperor wanted] to go to pray to this Buddha. At the appropriate period he twice sent some men ordering them to check if the ice on the river had frozen solid. When they came back reporting that the ice was not frozen solid, he killed them all. The men who were sent the third time the third time wept bitterly saying: "If we report that the ice is not frozen, we will be killed; if we report that it is frozen, when it isn't, how will we

Furthermore [I] read in the book on the history of our Dynasty: There was a progenitor of the Jin emperors, [...] [...] the Eastern territory, which was completely under his rule. But he did not like being an Emperor.

He heard about a Buddha in the western territories and he wished to go and to pray to [this] Buddha. He sent some men to check if the river was frozen; when they came back reporting that it was not frozen, he beheaded them. Again he sent some men to see, and when they came back reporting that it was not frozen he beheaded them [too]. Again he sent some men to check, and when they saw that the river was not frozen, they wept bitterly on the river's bank. Now, a dragon king in human features apppeared; after he had spoken with the men, he ordered them to go back and to report that the riv-

我有皇[ ]統為帝
祖鼻東方[ ]盡屬不願
觀史書
又
9a 又觀國史書金鼻帝馭

有求燠江回即使之視江未凍哭泣龍人作與令江凍
聞西方佛欲往佛時尚使人視水凍報未斬之又人回報未斬之又使人之見江凍邊王
9b 形者語回報江已凍

bi seme alanajina seme hendure jaka de amasi jūhe jafahabi seme alanabi han **33** geneci aihōma hurui kio cahabi: han neneme doobi amasi tuwara wara jaka de aihōma gemu mūkede dosibi kio efujebi hōwa bahabi doohakōbi:	die?" A dragon king appeared, transformed himself into a man, and said, after having asked them [why they were weeping]: "You will die even if you lie; so report that the ice is frozen solid." At their return they reported that the ice was frozen solid. When the Khan went there, turtles had made a bridge with [their] shells. When the Khan had crossed first and looked back, all the turtles submerged, destroying the bridge. Having reached the opposite [bank], he could not cross [the river again].	er was already frozen. When the Emperor came to the river, turtles had made a bridge [with their] shells. The Emperor crossed the river, but when he looked back turning his head, [he saw] that the turtles suddenly submerged and nobody could cross the river.

上橋江至帝
橋成背龜
江過帝渡
視一首回
滅倏橋龜
濟得不眾

tereci han emhun fūcihi be baime genehebi: amala han-i doro lakcabi.	After that, the Khan went alone to pray to Buddha. Later he lost [his] Imperial power.	So the Emperor went alone to the western territories to pray to Buddha. Later he lost [his] Empire.

西往自帝
遂佛求方
失天下

terei kadalaha sū ui: be do: anguce: fūniẏe: hoosi: hešui: be šan: **34** seme nadan gūrun-i niẏalma balai samsihabi: han seme banjire de elerakō: fūcihi be baime genehe be abka wakalabi han-i doro akcaha koo-	The seven tribes under his rule, the Suwei, Bedo, Anguce, Funiye, Hoosi, Hešui and Be Šan, scattered everywhere. It is not enough in life simply to claim to be an Emperor. Heaven disapproved of his going to pray to a Buddha, [and therefore] he forfeited the Imperial rule. This is the sixth	The seven tribes under his rule, the Suwei, Boduo, Anguche, Funie, [Haoshi], Heishui, Beshan and other peoples all scattered over mountains and valleys. He did not like being an Emperor and his only desire was to pray to Buddha. Heaven's wish was to reproach him and so he lost the Em-

七練所其
伯未粟部
車骨安咄
[ ][ ]涅拂
山白水黑
皆民人等
谷山伏竄
為願不矣
意一而帝
天佛求**10a**
遂之怪心
此下天亡
也六其

6th example

li ere ninggun: example.   pire. This is the sixth [example].

Comment

With this example Nurhaci opens the section on the Jurchen Jin 金 dynasty (1115–1235), which he considers an "ancient Manchu state" (*julge manju gurun*). This definition is missing in the Chinese version. He reveals that he took the example(s) from "the book of our dynasty" or, in the Chinese version, from "the book on the history of our dynasty". This "book" is identifiable with the *Jin shi* 金史, the oldest title for which in Manchu simply reads as "Aisin [gurun]-i *kooli*", and was later changed in "Aisin gurun-i *suduri* [*bithe*]".[1] Nurhaci probably had to consult its Chinese version, since the Manchu translation was ordered in 1635 and was only published in 1646.[2] But as is seen in the *JMZD* [I, p. 193), Nurhaci had used the *Jinshi* as early as 1616 when, after declaring war on the Ming, he taught his officials from "the history 'created' (i. e. written down) by the ancient Aisin khans": *julgei aisin han-i banjiha koolibe alabi*.

The expression "Primordial progenitor of the Jin" (Jin Bizu 金鼻祖), used in connection with the territory of the Mohe tribes, is also found in the 9th chapter of the *Manzhou yuanliu kao* 滿州源流考;[3] in its Manchu version (*Manjusai da sekiyen kimcin*, IX, p. 50a) it reads *Aisin gurun-i deribuhe mafa* – "Primordial ancestor of the Aisin state". The source quoted there is the *Yuanshi, Dilu zhi* 元史地里志, under *Kaiyuan lu* 開元路 ; in the identical sentence quoted from the *Yuanshi* 元史 (*Manzhou yuanliu kao*, cit., XIII, p. 200) the characters Bizu 鼻祖 have been changed into Shizu 始祖, and correspond in the Manchu version (p. 4a) to *Aisin gurun-i da mafa* – "First Ancestor of the Aisin state". The *Shizu* of the Jin State is Wanyan Hanpu 完顏函普 (ca. 900): cf. Hok-lam Chan, *Legitimation in Imperial China. Discussion under the Jurchen-Chin Dynasty (1115–1234)*, Seattle-London 1984, p. 217.[4]

---

1   Fuchs, *Beiträge*, p. 124.
2   *Ibid.*
3   Ed. Sun Wenliang 孫文良 et. al., Shenyang 1988, p. 122.
4   The names of the seven Mohe tribes are listed, among other sources, at the beginning of the first chapter of the *Jinshi*, translated by A. G. Maljavkin, "Czin'-ši. Glava 1-ja, perevod s kitajskogo", in *Sbornik naučnych rabot prževal'cev*, Harbin 1942, pp. 41–58; H. Franke, "Chinese Texts on the Jurchen II. A Translation of Chapter One of the Chin-shih", in *Zentralasiatische Studien*, 12 (1978), pp. 413–452 [415–427]. For the distribution of the Mohe tribe see J. Reckel, *Bohai*, Wiesbaden 1995, (Aetas Manjurica 5), pp. 453–458. According to Korean sources, the seven Mohe tribes scattered after the destruction of Gaoguli in 668: see E. von Mende, *China und die Staaten auf der koreanischen Halbinsel bis zum 12. Jh.*, Wiesbaden

26

[7th example]

Manchu	Translation 1	Translation 2	Chinese
○ jai geli meni gūrun-i kooli be tuwaci:	Furthermore [I] read in the book of our Dynasty:	Furthermore [I] read in the book on the history of our Dynasty:	又觀我國史書
mini manju gūrun-i aguda gebungge niyalma: dailio han de dahabi: tasha lefu geoleme 35 wara: giyahōn maktara jūšen obi:	A man from my Manchu country named Agūda had served the Dailio Emperor, [living as] a Jušen, killing tigers and bears under cover and laun-ching falcons.	There were Aguda and his younger brothers Wuqimai, Nianhan and Hushe. They followed the Liao Emperor out hunting, knew how to call deer and catch tigers, to kill bears and to launch falcons.	有阿古打及弟吳乞買粘罕胡舍等嘗從遼主獵能呼鹿制虎搏熊放鷹
tondoi banjire niyalma be: sarin de maksi seci maksihakū tūrgun de waki sere jaka de: aguda nendehe aisin han-i samsiha gūrun be bargiyame beyebe dasara: ba be bekilere be:	When this upright man was ordered to dance during a banquet, and he refused to dance, [the Emperor] ordered him to be killed. For For this reason Agūda reunified the people of the country who had been dispersed by the former Aisin Khan, reigned himself and made [his] territory stronger.	He served the Liao Emperor, but when he waited once on the Liao Emperor during a banquet, and the Liao Emperor ordered all the tribal chiefs to dance, Agūda did not obey. Therefore [the Emperor] wished to kill this honest and upright man. Agūda rebelled, reunified all the people of the seven tribes dispersed by the Jin in former times, prepared cuirassed and repaired the fortifi-	奉事遼主嘗侍遼主宴遼主命諸酋起舞至阿古打不從欲將 10b 之公正無罪而殺之阿古打怨之遂合前金收部逃散七之眾繕甲修城

1982 (Sinologica Coloniensia 11), p. 63 footnote 210. For the geographical distribution see pp. 356–359 in H. Matsui, "Über die [sic] Verwaltungsgebiet des P'o-hai Reichs", in W. Yanai, I. Inaba, H. Matsui, *Beiträge zur historischen Geographie der Mandschurei*, Band I, Tokyo 1914, pp. 328–370. For a brief history see L. Gibert, *Dictionnaire historique et géographique de la Mandchourie*, Hongkong 1934, pp. 645–648.

For the "Dragon King" and its role in Chinese history and mythology see E. T. C. Werner, *A Dictionary of Chinese Mythology*, New York 1961, pp. 285–297.

7th example

dailio han donjibi: nadanju tūmen cooha gaibi ini beẏe genebi:	When the Dailiyoo Emperor heard this, he collected seven hundred thousand soldiers and moved against him.	When the Liao Emperor heard this, he personally lead seven hundred thousand soldiers to punish him.	遼主聞之親率兵七十萬伐之
aguda-i emu tūmen **36** cooha eterakū burlahabi: tereci aguda afaha dari dailio-i cooha be etebi dailio-i doro be bahabi: dailio han be jafabi wahakō: haibin wang sere beile obuhabi.	He could not win over Agūda's ten thousand soldiers and took to flight. Later Agūda defeated the Dailiyoo army and got the *Dao* of the Dailiyoo. After having taken prisoner the Dailiyoo Emperor, he did not kill him but made him a *beile* with the title Haibin Wang.	Aguda lead ten thousand soldiers and defeated the Liao army. Later he won many victories in many battles. Later he took the Liao Emperor prisoner and appointed him as Haibin Wang.	阿古打率兵一萬大敗遼兵從此屢戰屢勝遂獲遼主封為海濱王
tereci aguda amba aisin han-i gebu gaifi banjiha sere:	Later Agūda accepted the title Great Aisin Khan and [continued to] rule.	Later Aguda became the Jin Emperor.	阿古打遂為金皇帝
abka amba gūrun ajige gūrun seme ilgarakō: ūru waka **37** be tuwame tondoi beidehe kooli ere nadan.	Heaven does not distinguish between a great or small Empire, but only what is right and what is wrong and judges fairly. This is the seventh example.	Heaven does not distinguish between a great or small Empire; it considers only what is right and what is wrong and judges fairly. This is the seventh [example].	天之論事是非不大公斷其七也 國只**11a**之此
ere kooli be nikan si sarhōn:	This example, oh Chinese, didn't you know it?	How could your Southern Dynasty not know it!	爾南朝豈不知之
jasei tūlergi jušen gūrun-i niẏalma: nikan simbe aniẏa dari dūbe jecen be sūcubi gamame ehe facuhōn ban-	The Jušen people outside the border attacked the borderland every year and your Chinese [Empire]; they lived creating bad [sit-	In past years all the Yi outside the border sacked the fortified cities in your territory every year and took children and animals by force,	先諸夷搶地女民年邊年擄城牲不安爾內堡畜子士

7th example

Manchu	English	English	Chinese
jimbihe:	uations and] disorder.	there was no peace for the whole population.	世 出 朕 及 夷 諸 平 削 疆 邊 廷 朝 草 寸 動 不 土 尺
bi tucibi tere facuhōn be gemu nakabubi: han-i jasei orho bilgan akō: boigon sihabuhakū.	Then I appeared and put an end to all the disorder, without destroying any grass or soil of the Emperor's borderland.	Then We appeared and subdued all the Yi [people], without touching a blade of grass or a foot of soil of the Emperor's borderland.	
aniya dari han **38** de hengkileme tondo i banjire niyalma be: nikan si mini batangga yehei gisun be gaibi:	Getting rid of honest people who came every year to prostrate themselves before the Emperor, you, oh Chinese, believed the words of the Yehe, who are hostile to me.	Every year they came to the town with tributes, and lived in peace without interruption. But your Southern dynasty, be lieved the false words of [the people from] Beiguan, who are hostile to me.	歲 歲 修 貢 通 市 和 好 不 絕 而 爾 南 朝 聽 信 我 仇 人 北 關 誣 言
mini gūrun amban cooha geren ere be waci mini ciha dere seme tondo niyalma be waki sehebe abka simbe wakala bi sini gūrun-i joborongge dere kai:	When they said that it is my intention to kill them with my dynasty's great army's numerous soldiers, and you wanted [therefore] to kill me, an honest man, Heaven disapproved and will bring mischief on your Empire.	[When they said that] I, trusting in [my] dynasty's great army's numerous soldiers, would let them live or kill them according to my own discretion, you wanted to kill me, an honest and upright man without guilt. This will therefore provoke Heaven's disapproval.	自 侍 國 大 **11b**兵 眾 以 為 生 殺 由 己 欲 殺 我 公 正 無 罪 之 人 因 致 天 怪 也

Comment

The seventh example is again devoted to an episode from Jin history and concerns the well-known refusal of the Jurchen chief Agūda (1068–1124 [~1123?]) to follow the humiliating order of the Liao emperor to dance in front of him.[1] Parallels are made between the honest and loyal founder of the Jin (Aisin) State Agūda and the equally upright Nurhaci, founder of the Latter Jin (Aisin) State, who in the past went several times to Peking to pay respect and bring tributes to the Ming emperor. The

---

1   For this famous episode see *Wittfogel*, p. 409 and 422; *O. Franke*, IV, p. 184

episode of Agūdai's refusal is also recorded in the *JMZD* (I, 232-233) and underlines Nurhaci's claim to be considered the heir to the old Jurchen dynasty: not by chance the episode opens with the words "a man *of my Manchu country* named Agūda...", a sentence which is obviously missing in the Chinese version but which, however, also mentions Agūda's companions Ukimai (Agūda's younger brother and successor), Nianhan (= Niyanmoho) and Agūda's nephew Kushe.[2] Their insertion in the Manchu text was evidently considered a matter of no importance for the non-Chinese reader. An analogous but more stylistic difference is also seen when the text speaks about Agūda's proclamation as emperor: in the Manchu text, he became the "*Great Aisin khan*" (*amba aisin han*), while the Chinese text speaks about the "Jin emperor" (*Jin huangdi*). Furthermore, ethnonyms are given according to the respective language: to the Manchu "Jušen State" corresponds the Chinese "Yi 夷 ", and for the ethnically different readers' better understanding the Yehe tribe is usually called *Beiguan* 北 關 ("Northern Pass") in the Chinese version. Nurhaci is represented in this example as a man of "law and order", and at the same time obedient to the Chinese Emperor who, like the Liao emperor in the case af Agūda, "recompensed" him with hostile acts due to the Yehe's calumnies.

---

2   See H. Franke, "Chinese Texts on the Jurchen. A Translation of the Jurchen Monograph in the *San-ch'ao pei-meng hui-pien*", in *Zentralasiatische Studien* 9 (1975), pp. 119–186, esp. pp. 141 and 154.

[8th example]

○ jai geli donjici nikan-i sūng huišung **39** han-i fonde: dobi dosibi han-i besergen de tafabi tehebi: jai emu tūbihe unçara haha niẙalma beẙede obi jui ban jihabi: jai nūre unçara jū halangga niẙalmai sargan de gaitai andan de salu banjihabi: salu golmin juwan duin ūrhun bihebi:

terebe huišung han donjibi hehe doose obuhabi:

tere **40** huišung han: aisin han-i baha dailioi Jang Ku gebungge amban ubašame dosire jaka de alime gaibi: aisin han gaji seçi burakō dain obi: hui šung çinšung ama jui jūwe han be gemu jafabi: šanggiẙan alin-i çargi sunja gūrun-i heçen de falabume ūnggibi būçehebi:

Furthermore [I] heard: At the time of the Chinese Sung Emperor Huizung a fox came, climbed on the Emperor's bed and lay down. Furthermore, a man selling fruits became pregnant and gave birth to a son. Furthermore, the wife of a man called Ju, who sold wine, suddenly grew a beard. The beard was fourteen *urhun*[1] long.

When Emperor Huizung heard about it, he appointed her as a Daoist priestess.

[At that time] Emperor Huizung entertained a dignitary named Jang Ku of the Dailiyoo [Dynasty], who had escaped after having been captured by the Aisin Emperor; when the Aisin Emperor or[dered Huizung] to return him, he did not send him back. [Consequently a war broke out and the two Emperors, Huizung and Cinzung, father and son,

---

Furthermore [I] heard: At the time of Song Huizong, a fox climbed on the Imperial throne, a man gave birth to a child and a woman grew a beard.

By Imperial order she was appointed as a Daoist priestess.

At that time [the Song Emperor] entertained the Liao rebell Zhang Jue; the Jin people often asked in vain [for him], and this later provoked a war between the two Empires, during which the two Emperors, Hui and Qin, were captured. They were exiled to the City of the Five Nations in the White Mountain.

徽宋聞又
宗時狐
升御有
人坐男
人生子女
　生鬚

詔為女道
士

時叛
人納遼金
人張毀不
與索兩
國致執
徽兵二帝
欽爭
徙至白山
五國城

---

1   1 *urhun* = approximately 17 cm.

8th example

giran be jui gao-šung baire **41** jaka de amasi būhebi: umai ūile akō babi sain banjire gūrun de ūile araha be abka wakalabi ha<u>c</u>in ha<u>c</u>in-i ganio joribi: han-i beẙe jafabuha doro efujehe kooli ere jakūn:	defeated. They were exiled to the City of the Five Nations beyond the White Mountain, where they died. When the son Gaozung asked for [his father's] corpse, it was returned [to him]. Heaven disapproved that such a crime was committed against a peace-loving and guiltless country, and showed various kinds of omens. The Emperor himself was captured and lost his reign. This is the eighth example.	After their death, Gaozong asked for Huizong's corpse, which was returned [to him]. Provoking a battle with a peace-loving country, brought down Heaven's wrath. Calamities are often foretold. [The Emperor] himself was captured and the Empire destroyed. This is the eighth [example].	死後高宗 求徽宗 **12a** 尸還之 起釁生事 於無事之 國遂致天 怒災異屢 見身俘國 破 此其八也
nikan si mini ekisaka tondoi banjire niẙalma be waki se<u>c</u>i abka simbe wakalabi: ha<u>c</u>in **42** ha<u>c</u>in-i ganio joriha bikai: tere joriha ganio guwembio: abka sinde isibumbikai:	Oh Chinese, when you said that you will kill me, a peaceful and honest living man, Heaven disapproves of you and sends various kinds of omens. Can you ignore these omens? Heaven will deal with you!	I am by nature an honest and upright man, and your Southern Dynasty wishes to kill me without reason. This is what provokes the wrath of Heaven, and many calamities are sent down. How is it possible to escape? Finally, they will happen!	我本公正 之人爾南 朝欲平白 殺之所以 蒼天致異 屢降災乎 豈能逃矣 終必應矣

Comment

As already seen in the opening statement, this example once more refers to Chinese history and concerns the bad omens which appeared during the reign of the Song emperors Huizong 徽宗 (r. 1101–1125, † 1635) and his son Qinzong 欽宗 (r.

1126): a fox climbing on the emperor's bed,[1] a man giving birth to a child, a woman growing a beard.[2] Hostilities broke out between the Song and Jin dynasties in connection with the "traitor" Zhang Jue 張覺, whom the Song refused to extradite. The war ended with the Jin's victory and the consequent exile in 1130 of the emperors to the "City of the Five Nations", i. e. the city of Wuguo cheng 五國城, which is identifiable with present day Yilan east of Harbin.[3] Ignoring the warning omens, the Song waged an unprovoked war against a peaceful people the result of which was the fall of the Song. According to Nurhaci's conclusion, the same situation is repeating now between his reign and the Ming.

The puzzling element in this example is the name of Zhang Jue, the second part of which is written in the Chinese version with the unusual character 㲉 *jue*. According to H Franke,[4] however, the second character of the name should be written with the homophone 覺. In the *JMZD* the name is found as one word, Jangjiyoo, which in the *MWLD* has been corrected to Jang Giyo, the latter being the Manchu transcription of Chinese Jue: see *JMZD* I, 539 (= *MWLD* I, 233); II, 715 (= *MWLD* I, 352). The variant Jangjoo (*JMZD* II, 1126), corrected in Jang Giyo in the *MWLD* (II, 601), is also found. The compiler of the Manchu text read it as *Ku* or *Gu*[5] – a possible variant but clearly wrong in our context.

---

1   See J. J. M. De Groot, *Universismus*, Berlin 1918, p. 354: "Füchse haben den nahen Sturz von Kaisern dadurch prophezeit, daß sie sich in ihre Paläste und Privatgemächer eingeschlichen hatten". Several foxes appeared also when the last Yuan emperor Togon Temur escaped to the north, lying down under his throne (E. Haenisch, *Zum Untergang zweier Reiche*, Wiesbaden 1969, Abhandlungen für die Kunde des Morgenlandes XXXVIII/4, p. 36). See also J. J. M. De Groot, *The Religious System of China*, Leiden 1907 (repr. Taipei 1976), vol. V/II, pp. 576–600.

2   For the growing of beard and sex-mutation as bad omens, see De Groot, *Universismus*, pp. 350–351. For other examples in Chinese literature see K. De Woskin & J. I. Crump, Jr., *In Search of the Supernatural*, Stanford 1996, pp. 66, 76, 84 (taken from the *Soushen ji* 搜神記 by Gan Bao 干寶, 4th century).

3   For details, see *Wittfogel*, p. 92, and *Gibert*, p. 693. See also the entry *Wu-kuo-ch'êng* 五國城 (pp. 140–147) in H. Matsui, "Das Verwaltungsgebiet des Chin-Reiches in der Mandschurei", in H. Matsui, W. Yanai, I. Inaba, *Beiträge zur historischen Geographie der Mandschurei*, Tokyo 1912, pp. 115–205.

4   In his "Treaties Between Sung and Chin", in F. Aubin (ed.), *Études Song in Memoriam Étienne Balazs*, Paris 1970, pp. 55–84, and in the glossary on p. 82. (repr. in Franke & Chan, IV, same pagination). The same reading and character is also found in D. Thiele, *Der Abschluss eines Vertrages: Diplomatie zwischen Sung- und Chin-Dynastie 1117–1123*, Wiesbaden 1971, where large space is devoted to Zhang Jue's vicissitudes. For his life and destiny, see O. Franke, IV, pp. 204–212; V, p. 118.

5   The name "Janggu" is also found in the Guimet ms. 61625 (f. 96), and "Jangku" in the ms 61624 (f. 49): see the facsimile in Pang/Stary 1998, p. 149 and 224.

[9th example]

○ geli meni kooli be tuwa_c_i:	Furthermore [I] read in our book:	Furthermore [I] read in the book on the history of our Dynasty:	又觀我國史書
aisin gūrun-i aguda han-i ila_c_i jalan-i hišung dan han-i fonde amba edun dabi: gūrun-i boo efujebi wase moo niy̌alma ulha **43** juwan bai dūbe de isitala daribi niy̌alma ambula bū_c_ehebi:	In the time of Emperor Hizung Dan, the third generation of Agūda of the Aisin Empire, there was a great storm. The houses of the Empire were destroyed, and tiles, trees, people and animals were flung for a distance of ten miles. Many people died.	At the time of Emperor Xizong, three generations after Jin Taizu, one night there was a strong storm, rain, lightning and thunder, which destroyed houses and palaces; fire broke out in the bedrooms and burned the curtains. The strong storm also destroyed the houses of the [common] people and the habitations of the officers. Tiles, trees, people and animals, everything flung for a distance of more than ten miles. More than a hundred people were mortally wounded.	金世宗皇帝時風雨雷電震**12b**壞殿鴟尾入寢內火燒幛幔又壞民居官舍人畜皆木飄颺十數里死傷數百人
tuttu ganio joribi: hišung han: wan y̌an liy̌ang de wabuha sere: hišung han da de sain bihebi: dūbe de gōwaliy̌andara jaka de: abka wakalabi ganio joribi: bey̌e wabuha kooli ere uy̌un:	After such omens appeared, Hizung was killed by Wan Yan Liyang. Originally Hizung was a good Emperor; [but] at the end he changed. Heaven disapproved it and sent [these] omens. After that, he was killed. This is the This is the ninth example.	Many bad omens appeared, and at the end it was Wanyan Liang who killed him. Originally Xizong's rule was good; but since his nature changed latterly for the worse, Heaven sent down calamities and he was killed. This is the ninth [example].	屢降災兆完顏熙竟為所弒宗初政善其初因心天身弒災異身弒 此其九也

Comment

This very short example is, for the first time, the result of Nurhaci's "reading (*tuwaci*) of our book", which in the Chinese version corresponds to the "reading of the book on the history of your dynasty", i. e. probably the *Jinshi* 金史. The content is devoted to the third Jin Emperor Xizong [Dan 亶 (this character is missing in the Chinese text)], i.e. Hizung Dan in the Manchu version, and the bad omen sent by Heaven before he was killed by Wanyan Liang in 1149. Hok-lam Chan pointed out that the bad omen took the form of hurricane and lightning, which occurred in the 4th month of 1149 and during which "Lightning struck Hsi-tsung's residential palace and the bed caught fire".[1]

---

1 See p. 859 of his article "Calamities and Government Relief under the Jurchen", in *Papers on Society and Culture in Early Modern China*, Taipei 1992, pp. 781–872.

[10th example]

44 ○ geli meni kooli be tuwaci:	Furthermore [I] read in our book:	Furthermore [I] read in the book on the history of our Dynasty:	又觀我國史書
aisin gūrun-i aguda han-i duici jalan-i wan ẙan liẙang: hišung han be wabi han tehe manggi: ucimai han-i jūse omosi niẙanmoho-i jūse omosi be etuhun hōsungge seme: ini han tere onggolo daci ibiẙala [?] bihengge [?] **45** obi gemu wacihiẙame wahabi	Wan Yan Liyang, the fourth generation of Emperor Agūda of the Aisin Dynasty, ascended the Throne after having killed Emperor Hizung. Even before ascending the Throne, he was detestable from the very beginning [?], and since the sons and nephews of Emperor Ucimai and the sons and nephews of Niyanmoho were strong and vigorous, he killed all of them.	Wanyan Liang lived at the time of Xizong; seeing that all the sons of Taizong and all the sons and nephews of Nianmohe were strong and vigorous, he killed all of them after his accession to the Throne.	完顏亮在 **13a** 熙宗世諸 見太宗子 子粘沒喝 孫俱強 盛及即位 後盡殺之
tuttu wabi ūksun-i niẙalmai sargata be hōwa de dosimbuhabi	After having them killed, he installed the wives of the clan members in the palace.	He installed the wives of the clan in the palace.	納其宗婦於宮
jai udai gebungge jiẙeduse hafan-i sargan ding go be huwekiẙebubi: eigen udai be wabubi: ding go be fujin obuhabi:	Furthermore, he incited Ding Go, the wife of the military commissioner Udai to have her husband be killed, and [then] he appointed Ding Go as main concubine.	Furthermore, he incited Ding Ge to kill her husband, the virtuous military commissioner Wudai, and [then] he appointed Ding Ge as main concubine.	又使定哥 殺其夫崇 義節度使 烏帶以定 哥為貴妃
tereci ūksun-i sargan jūse be seme targarakō ohobi:	From that time on he did not show any restraint toward the clan's daughters.	He became unrestrained in [his] excesses, did not have any sense of shame toward the clan's	恣於淫洪 至於宗族 姪女無所 忌恥皆與

jai ūlu gebungge beilei sargan ūlin dase **46** gebungge fūjin be ganara jaka de: fūjin beilei baru hendume bi ganarakō oho de: beile simbe han wambi: mini be-y̌ebe bi sere seme genebi: liy̌ang hiy̌ang gebung-ge gašan de ini bey̌ebe i wahabi. tere wan y̌an liy̌ang han: jang jung ku gebungge amban-i baru hebešebi: da-habi banjire nikan gūrun be **47** babi sain de dailambi serede: amba eni-y̌e tusiy̌an taiheo tafulara jaka de eni-y̌e be wahabi: tere-ci ninju tūmen c̣ooha be tanggō tūmen seme algimbubi: fujisa be gamame nikan be dailame genehebi: tuttu a-limbaharakō os-hon ehe obi: ini amala: geren am-basa aċabi ūlu ge-bungge **48** beile be han tebubi:	Furthermore, when he called for Ulin Dase, the wife of a prince named Ulu, the wife told the prince: "If he cannot take me, the Khan will kill you, the prince. So I will decide." Saying that, she left for a village called Liyang Hiyang and killed herself. That Emperor Wan Yan Liyang conferred with a dignitary named Jang Jung Ku, saying that after the [partial] conquest [of Song] it would be good to attack the Chinese Empire which had survived. When the Great Mother Em-press Dowager Tu-šan warned him, he killed the mother. Then, bragging that his six hundred thou-sand soldiers were one million, he took the wives and went to fight against the Chinese. Since he was incredibly pet-ty and bad, all the dig-nitaries met after his departure for the war and appointed prince Ulu as Emperor.	nieces, and all had to be at his service. Furthermore, when he called for Wulin dashi, the wife of Wulu, a prince of the blood, Wulin dashi said to Wulu: "[If] I do not go, the Emperor will kill [you,] the prince. I will decide and not involve [you]". [Thereafter] she went to Liang Xiang and killed herself. Later he consulted with his dignitary Zhang Zhongke on conquer-ring the peaceful Em-pire of the Southern Song. When the Em-press Dowager Tushan warned him, he killed her. Then he took the concubines from the back part of the pal-aces, led six hundred thousand soldiers, asserting falsely that the number was one million, to fight a-gainst the Song. Since he was without a *Dao* and nobody want-ed to obey him, after the departure of the ar-my all the dignitaries appointed Wulu, a a prince of the blood, as Emperor.	之私又召葛王烏祿妻烏烏林答氏烏林答氏謂林答氏 **13b**祿曰上我不行王勉不殺自我當自相累也以行至良鄉自殺 又與其臣張仲議和伐軻南宋國好之徒單太諫之后弒不不於之從是後宮率兵妃六萬六姓十萬號百此稱如必宋眾伐大兵無眾臣道葛王烏 **14a**祿為後去帝共立

10th example

imbe dain genehe ba de ini ambasa waha sere: fudasihōn ehe jurgan be yabubi abka wakalabi beye wabuha kooli ere juwan.	On the way to the war his dignitaries killed him. Since disloyalty and malignity were [his] principles, Heaven disapproved of him and had him killed. This is the tenth example.	When Wanyan Liang's army reached Guazhou, his own subordinates killed him. Disloyalty and malignity became Imperial principles, [he was] licentious and cruel. Therefore Heaven disapproved of him, and he himself was killed in a foreign country. This is the tenth [example].	兵州所天暴天異十也 顏亮至瓜其下殺逆亂常貪淫虐以致身弒此其
han niyalma doroi jurgan-i gamarakō: beyei gōnihai gamaci abka ombio: nikan si abka be teburakō: sini beye be abka arabi: ūile akō niyalma be **49** babi waki seci abka simbe wakalabi sini gūrun-i joborongge dere kai:	If a man being an Emperor does not act according to moral principles, but according to his own thoughts, how could Heaven allow it! Oh Chinese, it is not you who created Heaven, but you consider yourself to be the Heaven. Since you wish to kill [me,] a man without guilt, Heaven disapproves of you and will bring misfortune to your dynasty.	If a man who becomes an Emperor does not follow moral principles, if he acts in a wrong way according to his own will, how could Heaven agree with this! Your Southern Dynasty is without Heaven and Earth, but you consider yourself to be the Heaven. To kill me, a man without guilt, is disapproved of Heaven's will, and therefore a riot will break out.	主理意豈乎 凡為人不順道任其私妄行天肯容之 爾南朝無天無地自以為天殺我無罪之人天心憚之受此禍亂也

Comment

This example is devoted to the murderer and successor of Xizong Dan, the fourth Jin Emperor Wanyan Liang (personal name Digunai 迪古乃, 1112–1161) – a "brute sanguinaire"[1] as can be seen from the description given by Nurhaci. Not surprisingly, Wanyan Liang ended up by being killed too, and Nurhaci saw in this event Heaven's punishment for the emperor's policy based on violence and lack of virtues: the same hate, Nurhaci argues, will be reserved for the Ming emperor who wants to kill him, and who is "not acting according to moral principles".

Noteworthy is the Manchu reading of the Empress dowager's name 徒 單 as Tušan (in the old orthography Tusiÿan), which in Western publications is usually given as Tu*dan*,[2] i.e. according to another possible pronunciation of the character 單 ; this reading seems to derive from the *Tukdan* clan to which the empress belonged (personal comunication of H. Franke). As in some foregoing examples, the Manchu text misses some historical details found in the Chinese version, as for example the name of the place (Guazhou 瓜 州) where Wanyan Liang was killed; on the other hand, the Manchu texts specifies, evidently to make it easier for the reader to understand, that "Liang Xiang", the place where Ulin Dashi committed suicide, is the name of a *gašan*, i.e. a "village".

---

1 Definition given by *Gibert*, p. 885, in the emperor's biography on pp. 885–886, who concluded by saying that "a cause de son inqualifiable conduite, il ne reçut pas de nom de temple. On lui donna plus tard le titre de Hai-ling Wang". For a different view see H. Franke, "The Hai-ling wang episode", pp. 239–243, chapter 3, "The Chin Dynasty", (pp. 215–320), in H. Franke and D. Twitchett (eds.), *The Cambridge History of China*, vol 6: *Alien regimes and border states, 907-1368*. Cambridge 1994. For Zhang Zhongke († 1159) see *O. Franke*, IV, p. 249 ("vagabundierender Gassenjunge"), and V, p. 135.
2 See H. Franke, *The Cambridge History of China* 6, p. 241,

[11th example]

○ geli meni kooli be tuwaci:	Furthermore [I] read in our book:	Furthermore [I] read in the book on the history of our Dynasty:	14b 又 觀 我 國 史 書
aisin gūrun-i aguda han-i sunjaci jalan-i ūlu han tehe manggi: daiding han seme gebuhebi:	When Emperor Ulu, of the fifth generation [descended] from Emperor Agūda of the Aisin Dynasty, ascended the Throne he was called the Daiding Emperor.		
daiding han aisin-i yaya han ci genggiyen bihe. sain niyalma be baitalame tafulara gisun be gaime: abkai fejergi taibin 50 obi: gūrun bayan irgen elgiyen banjihabi:	The Daiding Emperor was the most enlightaned of all Aisin Emperors. He employed good men, accepted words of warning and brought peace to the Empire. The Empire became rich, the people lived prosperously.	Emperor Shizong was the most enlightened ruler. He had a good understanding of the business of government, loved wise men, accepted warnings, brought peace to the Empire. The country granted richness to the people, public granaries abonded.	世 宗 皇 帝 最 為 文 明 之 主 明 達 政 事 好 賢 納 諫 天 下 太 平 家 給 人 足 倉 廩 有 餘
[................] [................]	[Text cancelled]	[Text cancelled]	[ ][ ][ ][ ] [ ][ ][ ][ ]
tuttu obi daiding han be ajige yoo siyōn sehebi:	Therefore Emperor Daiding was called the Little Yoo [and] Šūn [Emperor].	.... was called Little Yao [and] Shun [Emperor].	號 為 小 堯 舜
tondo sain be abka saišabi geren tūkiyebi han obi jalan halame onggorakō maktara kooli ere juwan nemu [sic].	Heaven praised his honesty and goodness, everybody lauded [him] and, after he became Emperor, he was remembrred by all generations who extolled [him]. This is the eleventh example	His rule was good and his conduct virtuous, he followed Heaven and took care of [his] subjects. For this reason, he became famous as an Emperor for thousands and ten thousands of generations after him. This	行 天 庶 為 善 政 懿 皇 臣 得 名 上 格 帝 揚 萬 世 下 服 於 千 之 後 此 其 是 以 皇 帝 十 一 也

is the eleventh [example].

Comment

This is one of the few cases Nurhaci quoted as an example of a virtuous emperor: it is the fifth Jin emperor Shizong 世宗 (personal name Ulu 烏祿, Chinese name Wanyan Yong 完顏雍, the Daiding 大定 Emperor, 1123–1189. r. 1161–1189), who was "dubbed by the Sung Neo-Confucian master Chu Hsi 朱熹 (1130–1200) as a *hsiao Yao Shun* 小堯舜 ("miniature of Yao and Shun") for his enlightened rulership".[1] It is noteworthy that only the Manchu text, at the beginning, specifies that Ulu was the emperor of the fifth generation, and that he was called "Daiding Emperor"; the Chinese version quotes him in the second sentence, but with the posthumous title Shizong.

For unknown reasons, eight characters of the Chinese text (f. 14b) have been cut out from the printing plate; they correspond to 1½ lines in the Manchu version (f. 50).

---

1 Quoted from p. 803 in Hok-lam Chan, "Calamities and Government Relief under the Jurchen Chin Dynasty", in *Papers on Society and Culture in Early Modern China*, Taipei 1992, pp. 781–872; H. Franke translated this "nickname" of the mythical emperors Yao and Shun with "Little Yao and Shun" (*The Cambridge History of China* 6, p. 244).

[12th example]

○ geli meni kooli be tuwaci:	Furthermore [I] read in our book	Furthermore [I] read in the book on the history of our Dynasty:	15a 又 觀 我 國 史 書
aisin gūrun-i 51 aguda han-i ūyuci jalan-i jangšung han de monggoi temujin dahabi tondoi alban bū- me hengkileme jihe niÿalma be banjiha arbun be tuwabi waki sehe tūrgun de dain o- bi: aisin han-i doro temujin de gaibubi temujin cinggis han-i gebu gaibi ban- jiha sere:	When Emperor Jang- zung, of the ninth generation [descend- ed] from Emperor A- gūda of the Aisin Dynasty, beheld the the appearance of the Mongol Temu- jin, a man who had submitted and who was prostrating him- self before him hon- estly paying trib- utes, he said that he should be killed; for this reason a war broke out and the rule of the Aisin Emperor passed over to Temujin. Temujin lived taking the name Cinggis Khan.	In the time of Empe- ror Zhangzong, there was the chief of a Mongol tribe, Tiemu- zhen, who faithfully brought the tributes. Looking at his extra- ordinary appearance, [Zhangzong] wished to kill him for no reason. Therefore a war broke out bet- ween the two Em- pires, and the [Ai- sin] Empire was lost to Tiemuzhen. Later Tiemuzhen pro- claimed the Great Yuan [Dynasty].	章 宗 皇 帝 時 有 孟 古 部 長 鐵 木 真 忠 順 進 貢 見 其 狀 貌 奇 異 無 故 欲 殺 之 以 致 兩 國 兵 爭 天 下 失 於 鐵 木 真 鐵 木 真 遂 稱 大 元
abka amba gūrun ajige gūrun seme ilgarakō ūru 52 waka be tuwame beidehe kooli ere juwan juwe:	Heaven does not dis- tinguish between a great or small Em- pires, but only what is right and what is wrong, and judges fairly. This is the twelfth example.	Heaven does not dis- tinguish between a great or small Em- pire, but only what is right and what is wrong, and judges according to right- eousness. This is the twelfth [example].	天 不 論 國 之 大 小 只 論 事 之 是 非 公 斷 此 其 十 二 也
nikan si ere kooli be sarhōn:	Oh Chinese, didn't you know this ex- ample?	How could your Sou- thern Dynasty not know it!	爾 南 朝 豈 不 知 之
sini daci banjiha tondo jurgan be gōwaliÿabi abka	You gave up your o- riginal righteousness, and Heaven disapproved.	Your Southern Dyn- asty changed your honest heart, and	爾 南 朝 改 15b 變 公 正 之 心 天 心

12th example

wakalabi amban be ajigen obume: geren be komso obume gamara be ulhirakō sini kemuni jase de <u>si-binjire</u> bithe de geli mini gūrun amban: <u>c</u>ooha geren: simbe amba alin-i umhan be gidara gese obumbi 53 seme hendurengge būton wajire ūnde obi hendure gisun kai:	of it. Making great things small, and frequent things rare, and clear things unclear, in your letters sent [?] to [my] borderland you always compared the great numerous army of my Dynasty to eggs, which are crushed by a great mountain and which symbolizes you. These are words pronounced before the register of deaths has yet been compiled.	the heart of Heaven disapproved. On purpose you are cutting great [things] making them small, diminishing numerous [things] making them few; you also [pretend] to understand [things] which you do not know; with reference to [your] great Imperial army, you compared yourself to a high mountain and me to a hen's egg, and foolishly you spoke about a great mountain which crushes a hen's egg. Since your register of deaths is not yet finished, your words are not realistic.
liodun-i hetu juwan inenggi ūndu juwan inenggi y̌abure ba de alin bigan de jaluki y̌ame bisire šanggiy̌an giranggi nikan sini amba alin-i gidaha umhan-i nothoo: tere <u>c</u>ooha komso biheo: geren seme abka <u>c</u>i gereōn; hūsun seme abka <u>c</u>i hōsunggeo:	Walking the length and breadth for ten days in Liyoodung, white bones are seen covering mountains and open fields. Are these the eggshells crushed by your great mountain? Was this army small? Was the number bigger than Heaven? Was the strength strongert than Heaven?	[Walking] the length and breadth for ten days in the territory of Liaodong, white bones exposed to the sun cover mountains and the soil. Are these the eggshells crushed by your great mountain? How was it possible to say that its number was a heavenly number, that its strength was a heavenly strength?
54 abka wakala<u>c</u>i tere geren bimbio: borhoho umiy̌aha	If Heaven disapproves, could it be numerous? It would be like living	It was Heaven which disapproved of it, and [such] a number and

削減爾覺國以比比如雞爾壓爾數盡不得爾言也

怪之故大為眾尚悟仍大兵太山以雞我妄太山卵不死數故由爾

遼東橫十十遍暴太16a的卵爾馬論天豈

地方直日山滿地白骨露是爾山壓耶時兵豈少豈眾眾論

天眾如力力所難支如天怪之力

be niçarame wara gese banjimbikai:	[for] killing and bruising accumulated insects!	strength could [therefore] not exist. It would be like killing and bruising accumulated insects; what kind of trouble is this!	將聚虫抹殺一樣有何難也

Comment

This example concentrates on the contrast between the Jin emperor Zhangzong 章宗 (1190–1208, r. 1190–1208, personal name Madage 馬達葛, Chinese name Wanyan Jing 完顏璟) belonging to the ninth generation of Agūda (a fact which is not mentioned in the Chinese version) and the young Temujin, the future Cinggis Khan of the Mongol empire. Noteworthy differences between the two versions are seen at the very beginning: the Manchu version only says that Temujin "took the name Cinggis khan" (*Cinggis han-i gebu gaibi*), while only the Chinese version reveals that he founded the "Great Yuan" dynasty. The offensive comparison between the "Great mountain" (the Ming army) which crushes eggs (Nurhaci's army) is also found in a sacrificial message prepared in 1630 by the second Manchu emperor Hong Taiji to be read at the tombs of Agūda (Taizu) and Ulu (Shizong),[1] and was also inserted in the *Huang Qing kaiguo fanglue* 皇清開國方略.[2] It is also worth noting that the Manchu word *sibinjire*, which is translated here by "sent" on the basis of its compound *-jire* (< *jimbi*, 'to come') is nowhere to be found.

---

1 See *JMZD* VI, 2942–2943.
2 Chapter XII, 13a; Manchu version (*Daicing gurun-i fukjin doro neihe bodogon-i bithe*) chapter XII, p. 52a. For a German translation, see *Hauer*, p. 218: "... wie der T'ai-shan einen Haufen Eier zermalmt".

[13th example]

Manchu	Translation 1	Translation 2	Chinese
○ jai geli donjici cinggis han-i ju-wan duici jalan-i togon temur han-i fonde cinju-i alin efujebi na fakcahabi: jai biyanliyang-i hecen de senggi agabi niyalmai etuhe etuku gemu fulgiyan icebuhebi:	Furthermore [I] also heard that at the time of Togon Temur Khan of the fourteenth generation of Cinggis Khan, in Cinju a mountain was destroyed and the earyh and the earth split open. Furthermore, blood was rained down in the city of Biyanliyang and dyed the clothes of the people red.	Furthermore [I] heard that at the time of the Yuan Emperor Shunzong in Qinzhou a mountain was destroyed and the earth split open. Furthermore, in Bianjing blood rained down and all the people's clothes were red.	又聞元順宗皇帝時秦州山崩地裂又汴京雨血人衣皆赤
jai han-i hecen-i 55 na ašabi jiming san alin efujehebi: na šiungkubi gomin tanggō ba de isitala omo obi niyalma ambula bucehebi: abka tuttu emdubei ganio sabi jorici ehebe halame sain jurgan be yabuhakō: jalingga ambasai gisun be dosibi: tondo ambasa be baitalarakō obi abkai fejile baba de 56 dain dekdebi: togon temur han-i doro efujehe sere: abkai joriha ganio jūrcehe akō efujehe	Furthermore, the earth trembled in Khan's city and Mount Jiming was destroyed. The earth got dented and a one hundred mile-long lake appeared. Many people died. When Heaven shows persistently omens and signs, [it means that] good duties are not carried out to change bad things. Since the words of wicked dignitaries were accepted, and upright dignitaries were not employed, wars broke out everywhere in the Empire. Speaking about the loss of Togon Temur's Empire: it was foundered because the omens	Furthermore, in the capital the earth trembled and Mount Jiming was destroyed. The earth got dented and a one hundred mile-long lake appeared. Many people died. Often when Heaven sends calamities, [it means that] it is not possible to make changes or to alter personal behaviour. [Since the ruler] listened to and believed knaves and did not employ trustworthy dignitaries, war broke out [and] the Empire was foundered. Heaven sent omens in advance, and it is impossible to escape [what follows]. This is why the Empire was foundered.	地山方成池 又京師地震雞鳴山崩地陷百 **16b** 里 人多沒死 天如此屢降災異不能改過自新 聽信奸人不用忠臣于戈蜂起遂失天下天預示兆不能逃終以失天下

13th example

kooli ere juwan ilan:	This is the thirteenth example.	This is the thirteenth [example].	此 其 十 三 也
ere kooli be nikan si sarhōn:	This example, oh Chinese, didn't you know that?	How could your Southern Dynasty not know that!	爾 南 朝 豈 不 知 之
sini liodun-i heçen -i hūçin de senggi tūçibi lio liodun-i heçen gaibuha kai: han-i tehe bejing heçen-i bira de jūwe aniya senggi eyebebi: amba **57** edun de eiten yamun de tebuhe sakda moo fūlehe suwaliyame ukçahabi: ūwehei paileo tura mokçohobi: abka joriha amba ganio be nikan si gūrun amban çooha geren seme abka de eljeme jailabuçi ombio: atanggi biçibe abkai gōnihadari ombi dere:	After blood came out from the wells in the city of Liodun, the city of Liodun was conquered. For two years blood flowed in the river of the Khan's capital, Bejing; because of a strong wind the old trees planted in all the Yamen were uprooted with their roots, the pillars of the stone gates were broken into pieces. Is it possible, oh Chinese, that you can rival Heaven, opposing the great omens sent by Heaven to your great Imperial army? No matter what will be, the Heaven's design shall prevail.	Blood came out from the wells in the city of Liaoyang, and soon Liaoyang was destroyed. In the city of Beijing, blood flowed in the Yu river for two years, a strong wind uprooted the trees in all Ya[men] and destroyed the pillars of the stone gates. Heaven portended great calamities, but how could the great Imperial army of your Southern Dynasty resst Heaven or have any influence on it? After all [Heaven's will] shall prevail.	遼 陽 城 井 中 出 血 北 陽 即 破 年 京 城 兩 流 玉 河 刮 血 **17a** 各 衙 內 老 樹 及 石 牌 樓 天 示 大 災 今 爾 南 兵 朝 眾 豈 能 違 天 而 移 之 乎 終 必 應 矣

	sent by Heaven did not lead [him] to change [his behaviour].		

Comment

The source of this example which has as its subject the last emperor of the Yuan dynasty, Togon Temur, should be different from the previous (*Jinshi*) one, to judge by the opening words:[1] In fact, Nurhaci "heard" (*donjici*) about the disaster and did not "read it in our book" (*mini kooli be tuwaci*), as he has done in the case of the examples concerning the Jin emperors. The bad omens announcing the fall of the Yuan dynasty, earthquakes, blood in the river, blood-rain and destructive storms, are now happening again under the Ming emperor, evidently with the same significance. The earthquake which "destroyed" Mount Jiming took place on the 12th September 1368.[2] Blood-rain, a phenomenon already described in the Tang period, announcing Togon Temur's flight and the fall of the Yuan dynasty is also found in Saγang Sečen's "Erdeni-yin tobči".[3]

The two versions differ from each other in some details: the Manchu version speaks about "Togon Temur Khan, the fourteenth generation of Cinggis Khan", which corresponds in the Chinese version to "Yuan Emperor Shunzong"; Bianjing (i. e. Kaifeng) is called Biyanliyang, and Liaoyang, which was conquered on 12th May 1621, is mentioned with its Manchu designation of that time, i.e. Liodun (= Liyoodung = Liaodong). Furthermore, only the Chinese version gives the name of the river in Peking where blood flowed, the Yuhe 玉河. The episode is copied word for word from a document in the *JMZD* (II, 1124) on a date corresponding to the 16th May 1622:

> *sini liodun-i hecen-i hōcin de senggi tūcibi: liodun-i hecen gaibuha*: "After blood came out from the wells in the city of Liodun, the city of Liodun was conquered."

The same document (II, 1125) registers the blood flowing in the capital's river, specifying also the date when it took place:

> *becing hecen-i bira de suwaẏan morin aniẏa duin biẏade emgeli. honin aniẏa dūin biẏade emgeli juwe jergi senggi eẏehe*: "In the river of the city of Becing, once in the fourth month of the yellow-horse-year [1618], and once in the fourth month of the [following] sheep-year [1619], blood flowed twice."

This information is followed (*ibd.*) by the description of the devastating storm which we find almost word for word again in this example:

---

1 The history of the Yuan Dynasty, from Cinggis khan till Togon Temur, was well-known at Nurhaci court at latest in 1620, as can be seen from a document transcribed in the *JMZD* of that year (I, 540–542).

2 E. Haenisch, *Zum Untergang zweier Reiche. Berichte von Augenzeugen aus den Jahren 1232–33 und 1368–70* Wiesbaden 1969, p. 30: "In dieser Nacht stürtzte der Nordwestgipfel des Ki-ming-shan zusammen mit einem Krach wie ein gewaltiger Donner...".

3 See Sagang Sečen, *Geschichte der Mongolen und ihres Fürstenhauses.* Herausgegeben und mit einem Nachwort von Walther Heissig, Zürich 1985 [rep. of I. J. Schmidt's translation, St. Petersburg-Leipzig 1829], p. 152

amba edun de ẙamun ẙamun-i amba moo fulehe suwaliẙame ukcaha: uwehei pailu mūkcoho sere: "Because of a strong wind the old trees planted in all Yamen were uprooted with their roots; the pillars of the stone gates were broken into pieces."

According to ms. Guimet 61625 this storm broke out in the red-dragon year 1616 (see Pang/Stary 1998, p. 44).

The *JMZD* can therefore be identified as the source for the compilation of the second part of this example.

[14th example]

58 ○ jai geli donjici: nikan gūrun-i jū iuwanlung gebungge niyalma: ajigan de ama eme juwe ahōn gemu akō obi emhun beye howašan obi giohame yabume hooju hecen de dosirede: duka jafaha niyalma jafabi wambi sere be hecen-i ejen sabi ūjihebi: tuttu jobobi amala abkai erin isinjibi han ohobi: emhun fusihōn **59** tondo be tuwarakō: erdemu be tuwame: abkai ūwehiyeme ūwasimbuhe kooli

Furthermore [I] also heard: A man of the Chinese Empire named Ju Iuwanlung lost his father [and] mother, and two elder brothers. Being alone, he became a monk. When he, wandering and begging, entered the city of Hooju, the gate keeper seized him and said he would kill him; when the lord of the city knew that, he cherished him. After a poor life, the moment determined by Heaven came and he became an Emperor. Heaven promotes without taking into account whether a man leads a solitary and humble life but only in regard to his righteousness and virtues.

Furthermore [I] heard: A certain Zhu Yuanlong of the Southern Dynasty had lost [his] father, mother and the elder brothers when he was small. Being an orphan, he became a monk. Begging for food, he arrived at Haozhou. The gatekeeper wanted to seize and kill him. The lord of the city, Guo Guangqing, set him free and cherished him. Later he got the Mandate of Heaven and became an Emperor. Heaven was not influenced by his being an orphan and poor but only took account of his virtues. Protecting him tacitly, he made him an Emperor.

朝者母身食而主釋之歸天不論祐帝
南龍父孤僧乞門養命為天貧惟默
聞元失弟為州執城光天遂子其獨德
又朱幼兄至濠欲殺郭而後之**17b**論孤其為

ere juwan duin:

niyalmai ciha oci togon temur han-i doro ai de efujembi: giohame yabure jū iuwanlung ai de bahabi han tembi: abka

This is the fourteenth example.
If it were left to the will of men, how could Togon Temur Khan lose the Empire! How could the itinerant beggar Ju Yuwanlung get it

This is the fourteenth [example].
If it were left to the will of men, how could Yuan Shundi lose the Empire! How could Zhu Yuanlong, a beggar, get an Empire! Obviously it was determined by Heav-

四心天失乞何天
十其人帝以龍人下
其依順元之得由
此也若元下朱食以可見

ūwehiẏeme aisi-lame han ohobi: abkai ciha se-rengge dere kai:	and become an Emperor! He became an Emperor because Heaven suported and helped him. This was Heaven's will.	en and not by men.	不由人也

Comment

The extraordinary life and destiny of Zhu Yuanzhang 朱元璋, who in 1369 proclaimed the Ming dynasty and became its first Emperor with the title Hong Wu 洪武, (1368–1398) is given here as an example of the rise of a poor man to become emperor – if he is supported by Heaven. Needless to say that Nurhaci identified himself with the same destiny.[1] Incomprehensible and inexplicable at first glance is the name by which he is referred to – Zhu Yuan*long* instead of Zhu Yuan*zhang*. According to Hok-lam Chan (personal communication) this name is first found in the 16th century novel by Hou Dian 侯甸, *Xiqiao yeji* 西樵野記, was then quoted by the author/compiler of the *earliest* edition (1591) of the *Yinglie zhuan* 英烈傳, but removed in all successive editions. This fact reveals that the compiler of Nurhaci's proclamation used not only historical works but also popular novels as a source. It is interesting to note that the founder of the Ming dynasty is referred to by this phantasy name also in the *JMZD* in a letter by Nurhaci dated 1623, as having been substituted for its right form in the *MWLD* of the Qianlong period.[2] A similar situation is found in the Chinese text in the case of the military commander Guo Zixing 郭子興, who is referred to as the "lord" (*ejen* / *zhu* 主) of the city of Haozhou, and who saved Zhu Yuanzhang's life by accepting him into the ranks of his rebel army against the Mongols. In our Chinese text he is referred to as Guo Guangqing 郭光卿, the same name under which he appears in the above-mentioned *Yinglie zhuan*.[3] The name is omitted in the Manchu version.

---

1 On the legitimation process concerning Zhu Yuanzhang see Hok-lam Chan, "The 'Song' Dynasty Legacy: Symbolism and Legitimation from Han Liner to Zhu Yuanzhang of the Ming Dynasty", in: *Harvard Journal of Asiatic Studies* 88.1 (2008), pp. 91-133

2 See *JMZD* V, 2041, and *MWLD* II, 760. The *JMZD* entry reads: *ju iuwanlung-i beye ama eme akō emhun giohame yabubi. goo yuwanšuwai fejile takōrambume banjifi*: "Ju Iuwanlung, having lost [his] father and mother, gad around lonely as a beggar. [Later] he lived as a follower under the paramount leader Goo."

3 See the entry "Kuo Tzu-hsing" by R. Taylor in L. C. Goodrich (ed.), *Dictionary of Ming Biography 1368–1644*, I, New York-London, 1976, pp. 777–780.

[15th example]

60 ○ geli meni gūrun-i kooli be tuwaci:	Furthermore [I] read in the book of our Dynasty:	Furthermore [I] read in the book on the history of our Dynasty:	又觀我國史書
manju gūrun-i beise aisin han ci ebsi gōwa encu gūrun be takabuhakō bicibe: manju gūrun-i teile ba ejelebi banjimbihe:	The *beise* of the Manchu reign did not have contacts with other countries since the time of the Aisin Khans. They only ruled over the Manchu state and lived there [in peace].	Since the time of the Great Jin, [our ancestors] did not rule over the whole country, but were constantly the rulers of [our] homeland.	以本國常為君 18a長 自大金後雖未統諸國而國之中
jūšen-i giyaho-i nadan jui gemu hōsungge mangga ban jibi: uksin etuhei uyun ihan-i dabali fekūmbihe:	The seven sons of a Jušen named Giyahu were strong and vigorous; once they put on the armour and [were able to] jump over nine oxen.	There were seven sons of Jiahu, belonging to the tribe of [our same] people who were all very strong. With their armour on, they were able to jump over nine oxen in a row.	人生俱能跳 有屬部者 賈胡七人大力連 子披甲九牛
tuttu beyebe mangga **61** hōsungge seme mūjilen den obi: ninggutai beisei sunjaci mafai ūrun be usitaha seme ninggutai beise cooha genebi giaho-i [sic] enen hōncihin be gemu waha: beye be mangga hōsungge seme: babi sain niyalma de necime ūile araha be: abka wakalabi ene-n hōncihin gemu wabuha kooli ere tofohon:	Since they were strong and vigorous, they became arrogant. When they took away the daughter-in-law of the fifth Ningguta beise by force, the Ningguta Beise came with soldiers and killed all the descendants of Giyahu. Heaven disapproved of those who were strong and vigorous and committed a crime against good men; [therefore] all descendants were killed. This is the fifteenth example..	Using their strength they took away by force the daughter-in-law of [one of] my ancestors. The ancestors became infuriated and sent [their] soldiers to annihilate the whole clan. Jiahu's family rested upon the brothers' arrogant forces and provoked themselves and without any reason [their] ruin. Heaven's will disapproved of it and put the whole clan to death. This is the fifteenth [example].	力之剿氏起心族其 恃將兒我發盡族恃豪無禍盡 其我婦祖兵誅賈其強自天怪十 祖搶怒征其胡兄有故之之死五 也

Comment

With this example Nurhaci opens the chapter of his ancestors' and his own history and life. He "read" (*tuwaci*) the episode in "the book of our dynasty" (*meni gurun-i kooli / wo guo shu*), which should be identified with an earlier version of his "Veritable Records" (*Yargiyan kooli / Shilu*). Unfortunately, no other Manchu sources such as the *JMZD* are available for this period. The episode about Giyahū's seven bullying sons is found in the first chapter of the *Manzhou Shilu* (*MZSL*) and in a recently discovered "draft version" (an earlier version of the *Shilu*?)[1] of Nurhaci's and his ancestors' actions, where we read:

Draft version : Giyahoi nadan haha jui gemu erdemungge mangga:
MZSL : Giyahū gebungge niyalma nadan haha jui gemu gabsihiyan hūsungge ofi:
Proclamation: Giyaho-i nadan jui gemu hōsungge mangga banjibi

Draft version :   ūksin etubi uyun ihan-i dabali fekūmbi
MZSL: uyun ihan be ilibufi uksin etuhei dabali terkime fekumbihe
Proclamation: uksin etuhei uyun ihan-i dabali fekūmbihe

As can immediately be seen from this comparison, the text of the proclamation is obviously closer – but not identical – to the "draft version". The "book" Nurhaci presumably read is therefore a compilation probably made by Erdeni bakši, about whom the *JMZD* in 1618 noted that "he wrote the book(s) recording the *kooli* (historical events)" – *kooli be ejeme bithe araha*.[2]

Nurhaci's ancestors, the heroes of this episode, are quoted as "Ningguta beise"[3] only in the Manchu text; in the Chinese version they are simply called *zu* 祖, "ancestors", because the reader would probably not know of them.

---

1 Facsimile publication by Matsumura Jun 松村潤, *Sin Taiso jitsuroku no kenkyū* 清太祖實錄の研究, Tōkyō 2001 (Tōhoku Ajia bunken kenkyū sōkan 東北アヅア文獻研究叢刊, 2); quotation from facsimile p. 10A.
2 *JMZD*, I, 211.
3 *Ningguta beise* (later: *beile*)" - the "Beile of the Sixes", were Giocangga (Nurhaci's grandfather) and his brothers Desiku, Liocan, Soocangga, Boolangga and Boosi. For this period see G. Roth Li "State Building before 1644", in W. J. Peterson (ed.), *The Cambridge History of China*. Vol. 9, Part One: *The Ch'ing Empire to 1800*, pp. 9–72, esp. p. 26–27.

[16th example]

62 ○ jūšen-i uÿun tai niÿalma uksun geren hōsungge seme ninggutai beisei sargan jui be eigen de benere be jugōn tosobi gaijara jaka de: ninggutai beise cooha genebi: uÿun tai enen hōncihin be gemu waha: mangga hōsungge seme babi sain niÿalma de ūile araha be abka waka labi: enen hōncihin **63** gemu wabuha kooli ere juwan ninggun:	The members of Jušen clan Uyunta, being all very strong, blocked the road and kidnapped a daughter of the Ningguta beise on the way to her husband. The Ningguta beise came with soldiers and killed all the descendants of the Uyunta. Heaven disapproved of those who, being strong, committed a crime against simple good men, and had all descendants killed. This is the sixteenth example.	Among a tribe of [our same] race there were nine brothers who were all violent and strong. When a woman of my ancestors' family was sent to her groom's house to be married, used force and kidnapped her on the road and took her away. My ancestors became infuriated and ordered many soldiers to annihilate the whole clan. Using their strength [the Uyunta clan] committed a crime without any son. Heaven disapproved of it and put the whole clan to death. This is the sixteenth [example].	**18b** 又屬部人有兄弟九人者皆猛烈好漢時我祖宗之女送嫁于夫家彼恃其勢強要劫于途中而奪之我祖大怒率兵征剿盡誅其宗族自恃豪強無故起釁天怪之一族盡死此其十六也

Comment

This brief example is a continuation of the episode described in the 15th example and is devoted to the successful, because just, expedition of the *Ningguta beile* against the Uyunta clan, who kidnapped one of the Beiles' daughters on the way to her groom. In the aforementioned "draft version"[1] this episode is told in richer detail than in the *Manzhou Shilu*, and the example itself is a condensed version of it.

---

1   For the text see *Matsumura Jun*, facsmile f. 9b–109a; according to the author, "Uyunta" should be understood as a clan name and not as "those who ruled by nine", as the Chinese text of the example suggests (see Matsumura Jun's transcription and Japanese translation on p. 56).

[17th example]

○ jai y̌ehei niy̌alma hendume meni y̌ehei jūwe hoton hada: ula: hoifa: monggo: meni beise geren: gūrun ambula: sini manju gūrun de atanggi beile bihe: sini emu bey̌e etukui emu tohon lakcaha gese kai: sinde ai bi seme hendume hada: y̌ehe: ula: hoifa: monggo **64** acabi mini umai ūile akō niy̌almabe babi waki seme cooha jihe: abka mimbe ūrulebi:cembe wakalabi ceni gūrun be minde būhe: abka geren komso be tuwahakū: ūru waka be tuwame tondoi beidehe kooli ere juwan nadan:	Furthermore, a Yehe man said: "Our two Yehe cities, the Hada, Ula, Hoifa, Mongols, and our Beise are numerous, the countries are big. When did your Manchu state have a Beile? You are like a button broken off from your dress. What do you have?" When the Yehe, Ula, Hoifa, and Mongols came together and sent the troops to kill me, a man without any guilt, Heaven supported me and disapproved of them: their realms were [therefore] given to me. Heaven does not distinguish between a great or small [Empire], but only what is right and what is wrong, and judges fairly. This is the seventeenth example.	Furthermore, a man from the Northern Pass said: "Our two cities of the Northen Pass, together with [the people of] the Southern Pass, the Ula, Huiba, and Mongols, are a great number of countries, and the princes are numerous too. Where are the princes of your Jianzhou? Being alone, you are like a button broken off from the dress. What difficulties do you have!" When [the people from the Northern Pass] joined with the Southern Pass, with the Wula, Huiba and Mongols, and came together with their soldiers, they wanted to kill me, a man without guilt. Heaven disapproved of it and protected me; therefore all the countries were given to me. Heaven does not consider if an army is great or small; it only considers if a deed is just or unjust, and judges according to righteousness. This is the seventeenth [example].

19a 又說我二關北灰扒也那長身依一之合剌古來無天而將賜論寡之斷七

關北兼剌古君你有一譬一斷何因關扒兵殺之彼遂國不眾事公其十

北關我城兀孟多多州長子紐般有南兀孟共我人天祐我**19b**諸我之只此也

北關我二城兀孟多多那你子服子一合剌古來罪怪我國諸天之兵是也

17th example

Comment

This example is part of Nurhaci's personal biography and was recorded in the *Manzhou Shilu*, probably on the basis of original Manchu documents now lost. The content refers to the joint attack of Jurchen and Mongol tribes against Nurhaci in October 1593 and his victory at Mount Gure over this numerically superior enemy. The identification of this battle is possible thanks to the following example, where it is told that the *beile* of the Ula tribe, Bujantai, was taken prisoner during the fighting.[1] As in the two preceding examples, the Chinese version must be a translation from a Manchu source, and its terminology had to be changed according to the Chinese ethnic and geographical knowledge of the area: indeed, in the Chinese version the Yehe are therefore called the "Northern Pass", the Hada – the "Southern Pass". "Manju Gurun" is translated by Jianzhou (Nurhaci's homeland), the Hoifa tribe by "Huiba".[2]

---

[1] For the description of the battle, see *Hauer*, pp. 25–27: "Sieg über die Krieger von neun Stämmen der Yehe, Hada und anderer am Berge Gure".

[2] For the different terminology (Northern~ Southern Pass, Hada etc.) see D. Heuschert, "Die Hada-Jurchen nach dem *Wanli wu gong lu* des Qu Jiusi", in G. Stary (ed.), *Materialien zur Vorgeschichte der Qing-Dynastie*, Wiesbaden 1996, pp. 23–51.

[18th example]

[O] ere dain de ulai gūrun-i bujantai be jafabi ūjibi amasi 65 ini ulai gūrun de ūnggibi: mini sargan jui be būbi hojihon obubi han oho manggi: ūjihe ama minde gōwaliyabi mini yabuha yehei sargan jui be gaimbi siherire [?] jaka de geli mini juwe sargan jui be būhe:

tuttu ilan sargan jui be būci ojorakō geli ineku yehei 66 sargan jui be gaimbi seme dain ojoro jaka de abka wakalabi: bujantai gūrun be minde būhe: bujantai beye yehe de genebi abka waha. yai-a ehe waka be abka sambi serengge dere kai: ere juwan jakōn:

During that war, Bujantai of the Ula state was captured; after having fed him, [I] sent him back to his Ula state. I gave him a daughter and made him [my] son-in law. After he a khan, his attitude towards me, the father who cared for [him], changed. When a marriage with a Yehe women, who had been promised [to me], was blocked [?], I gave him two of my daughters.

But he said the didn't want to marry three women but take [only] the Yehe woman. Therefore a war broke out: Heaven disapproved of [him] and gave Bujantai's realm to me. Bujantai itself went to the Yehe, [where] Heaven had him put to death. Heaven really knows all the bad things and outrages. This is the eighteenth example.

When during the battle I captured the Wula chief Bujantai, I fed him and sent him and sent him back to his homeland. Furthermore, I gave him a woman in marriage. Later he became the ruler of the Wula state. [Then] he forgot my great favours, changed his mind and rebelled. When the marriage with an old woman from the Northern Pass, which has been promised [to me], was blocked, I gave him two [other] women.

Bujantai sent the two women back and wanted to marry the old woman from the northern Pass. Heaven disapproved of his ingratitude and gave his realm to me. Bujantai escaped to the Northern Pass, where Heaven had him put to death. Surely Heaven can distinguish between good and bad. This is the eighteenth [example].

時兀剌酋
長卜占台
者我於陣
間孥獲養
之送歸本
國仍以女
嫁之後為
兀剌國王
忘我大恩
心背叛
挾我已
娶北老
聘關將
女我又
二女嫁

還卜占台
20a要娶女
關老天背
怪其恩恩
將背賜
其他國台
我卜關
逃歸北
為天所殺
不論善
天必惡
此鑒之
也其十八

Comment

This episode opens without *birga*, which is clearly an oversight since at the end we read that it is the eighteenth example. It is devoted to Bujantai, who is said in the preceding episode to have been taken prisoner, but whose life was spared by Nurhaci. Bujantai's treacherous life, in part a consequence of his plotted marriage policy,[1] came to an end before 1620, after he had spent the rest of his life as a refugee among the Yehe who were destroyed in 1619. The Manchu text contains the unknown word *siherire*, probably < *sihelembi* "to hinder". Noteworthy is also the old form "ẏai-a" for "yaya".

---

[1] See Bujantai's biography in *Hummel* pp. 17–18, and *Hauer*, pp. 46–48. For a different version of Bujantai's "marriage policy" see p. 61 of M. Miranda's article "Das Dongyi Nurhaci kao", in G. Stary (ed.), *Materialien zur Vorgeschichte der Qing-Dynastie*, Wiesbaden 1996, pp. 57–63.

[19th example]

O abka gosiha seme mini mūjilen den ohokō niÿalma de emu tohomai [?] ūile arahakō: 67 tondoi banjire niÿalma be nikan si jasei tūlergi en‌cu gūrun-i ūile de dabi jing waki se‌ci bi abka de hab‌šabi nikan simbe dailara jaka de: abka simbe wakala‌ha mimbe ūrule‌he:	Although Heaven loves [me], my mind never became arrogant. I never committed the slightest [?] crime against anyone. You, oh Chinese, assisted a different country outside [your] border in its crimes and wanted to kill [me], a man leading an upright. life. When I reported it to Heaven and a war broke out with you, Heaven disapproved. of you and supported me.	Although I often got Heaven's protection, my mind never became arrogant. I never dared to cause mischief in any man's life. Your Southern Dynasty favoured a different country outside its border and wanted to kill me, an upright man. When I reported this to Heaven and soldiers were sent, Heaven without hesiteting disapproved of [your] Southern Dynasty and sup-. ported me.	朕 雖 厲 獲 天 祐 志 氣 未 在 人 上 不 敢 分 毫 生 事 公 正 之 人 爾 南 朝 偏 護 邊 外 他 國 要 殺 之 **20b** 方 昭 告 皇 天 而 起 兵 不 想 天 怪 南 朝 而 祐 我
tere‌ci nikan si: ai gelerakō mini ba‌ru iselehe seme: fūlehe fetehe wa‌ki seme: dehi tū‌men ‌cooha **68** wasimbubi ineng‌gi boljobi duin goloi tū‌cike bi‌he: abka ineku simbe wakalaha: mimbe ūrulehe:	Later you, oh Chinese, challenged me [asking] how could I dare to resist; [for this] you wanted to kill me down to my very bones. You sent fou r hundred thousand soldiers, who came on a fixed date on four roads. Heaven again disapproved of you and supported me.	Then your Southern Dynasty challenged me [asking] how could I dare to send troops to resist. The Middle Kingdom sent four hundred thousand soldiers altogether, who came on four roads with the intention of annihilating me down to my very bones. Heaven again disapproved of you and supported me.	於 是 南 朝 又 説 何 我 舉 兵 抗 拒 中 國 發 兵 四 十 萬 四 路 齊 進 意 欲 剪 滅 除 根 天 又 怪 爾 祐 我
geren komso ha‌ran waka: abkai haran serengge dere kai: ere ju‌wan uÿun:	The fact that a country is small has no significance; Heaven's will is decisive. This is the nineteenth [example].	What matters is not whether [your soldiers] are numerous or few, but what Heaven wishes. This is the nineteenth [example]. Great [Emperor] Shun	不 在 眾 寡 只 在 天 意 此 其 十 九 也 躬 耕 大 舜

19th example

who himself ploughed the fields, the village-chief Liu Bang, the beggar [Zhu] Yuanlong, they [all] got Heaven's Mandate and became Emperors. I myself am a descendant of the Great Jin [Dynasty]. How can I be ruled over by anybody! When Heaven's Mandate is given, then it is not a question if a state is great or small. Heaven alone [decides] to support [an Empire] and to assure its success.

邦龍歸帝大昜於命國勿扶也
劉元有 **21a** 本裔制天即小自之成
長食命為我之受或歸寡天之
亭乞天尚王金嘗人有之論而

Comment

In this last example the accusations against the Ming are less detailed and are based on the reproach that it supported a "different country" (*encu gurun*), this is, the Yehe tribe. The writer refers to the aggressive Ming invasion "on four routes", which led to the famous battle of Sarhū in 1619 and Nurhaci's great victory. The main difference between the two texts is found in the final part which mentions the most famous examples from China's past (emperor Shun, Liu Bang, "Yuanlong" [= Zhu Yuanzhang]. This part is found in the Chinese version only, while the Manchu version inserts it in the following section. The Manchu word *tohomai* is not found in any dictionary.

[Résumé]

O jūlgeci ebsi kooli be donjici: amba **gūrun banjire idu** wajici: han ambasa **69** liy̌eliy̌ebi doro be fudasihōn gama-: me bey̌ei waka be sarkō: cokto amba mūjilen jafahai efujehebi:

In the books handed down from oldest times [I] read: When the lifetime of a great Empire comes to an end, Emperors and dignitaries become confused, the government is carried out in a wrong way, personal faults are not felt, hearts are filled with great arrogance and destroyed.

There is [a saying] handed down from old times that a great Empire is considered to have come to an end, [when] rulers and dignitaries become confused, duties are carried out inaccurately and unwillingly, personal errors are not felt, and arrogance leads to mistakes.

來盡昏逆不驕失之
自古以大國數必君臣迷行事理亂常知其過泰以

ajige gūrun abkai erin isin jici: abka mūjilen bahabume: aga edun nimanggi gecen be erin acabume ai jaka be tookaburakō ūwesimbuhebi: eitereci abkai ciha kai:

When for a small country the [right] time decreed by Heavven comes, then Heaven enters the heart, rain and wind and frost coincide at the proper time, and all things are done in the right order without delay. This is the general will of Heaven.

But when a small state gets Heaven's Mandate; the duties are given priority, Heaven grants assistance, wind and rain and frost will come at the proper time. [Heaven] silently helps and assists [that state].

天動天之各至成
或小國明將歸念行事比啟翼風雨霜**21b**以時默助以也

ūsin tarime banjiha siy̌ōn: **70** gašan bosiokō liobang: giohame y̌abure jū iowanlung inu abkai erin isinjibi han ohobi kai: mini hōncihin amba aisin han seme banjihabi kai: ūwei fejile jūšen aha bihe: abkai erin isinjici ajigen komso

[Emperor] Šun who made his living ploughing the fields, the village-chief Liobang, the begging and wandering Ju Iowanlung, they [all] became Emperors when the time [decided] by Heaven came. I was born as a descendant of the great Aisin Em-

haraōn: ūwehiy̌eme ūjire abkai haran kai:	perors, how than could I be a jušen slave! When the time [determined] by Heaven comes, then it is not a question of a small [country with] a few people; to be raised and supported is [only] a decision Heaven could take.		

nikan si amba gūrun **71** seci: mederi gese onco: alin-i gese ašarakō mūjilen jafabi necin neigen-i banjici: abka simbe ainu wakalambi: abka be daburakō: fudasihōn mūjilen jafabi gūrun amban: cooha geren: simbe amba alin-i umhan be gidara gese obumbi serengge: abka de waka sabuha ambula obi: sini **72** angga be sinde saliburakō: hūtu ibagan-i angga obubi gisurembi kai:	Oh Chinese, in your heart your great Empire is wide like an ocean and stable like a mountain. If you live in peace, how could Heaven disapprove of you? But if you do not have regard to Heaven's [laws], if your heart is rebellious, if you say that your Dynasty is great, your soldiers are numerous, that you will be like a great mountain which crushes eggs, then Heaven will consider it a big crime. Those words speak of your arrogance, for which you are responsiblea, and they come from the mouth of a demon.	Your Southern Dynasty is a great Empire, in [your] heart it is wide like an ocean, so stable like a mountain. If you live virtuosly and selflessly, how could Heaven destroy your Empire? But if your heart is not pure, without [connection to] Heaven and Earth, if you send messages interfering with borderland [questions], always repeating that the great Imperial army will crush [me] like a great mountain crushes eggs, then Heaven will disapprove of this crime, considering it a big one by your Southern Dynasty. Your mouth is used, but it is not you who speaks; it is the mouth of a demon	大心朝南爾
			心上存若國
			寛天如海如
			動書海之山
			私無不不正
			爾插正無公
			心國來私天
			上如復甚天
			天泰説存下
			書等兵邊無
			大天衆無地
			泰朝如插不
			等使卵國正
			天由豈大常
			朝鬼非泰復
			使而爾等說
			由 故天兵
			鬼 不朝眾
			而 做使壓
			  口由山
			  説鬼言
			  之而怪
			  也 之
			     爾
			     爾
			     怪
			     言

alin bira be banji-buha: abka hono alin be tūkiẙebi niẙalma be gidaha kooli akō kai:	When mountains and rivers were created, Heaven made mountains high but without ordering them to crush men.	who sats these words. When Heaven created high mountains, Heaven did not give high mountains the order to crush men.	況者成無山理舉而此罪 太天也有壓爾動壓亂國 **22a**山之即人怎太卵言家山生天者能山如積受禍矣
nikan si adarame alin be tūkiẙebi umhan be gidambi: sini tuttu sūi isabume balai gisurere de abka wakalabi sini gūrun-i **73** joboronggge dere kai:	Oh Chinese, how can you make [yourself as high as] a mountain and then crush eggs? Perpetrating crimes and speaking unreasonably, you are decried by Heaven and provoke disasters for your Empire.	How can you make [yourself as high as] a big mountain, and then crush eggs? Speaking falsely and perpetrating crimes, you provoke disasters for the Empire.	
soosida-i bithe de henduhengge: ooliha niẙalma dain be anggai gidambi: aldangga saha manggi jilgan-i esukiẙembi:isinjime wajiha manggi niẙakōrabi baimbi: boo de isinjiha manggi coktolome gisurembi serengge	In the book *Soosida* [?] it is recounted: "A cowardly man fights against a warrior with his mouth; when he sees that he is far away, he shouts aloud. When [the enemy] comes closer, he kneels down and prays. When he returns home, he speaks arrogantly."	The *Xuantan baozang* says: "A silly mind fights against an enemy with his mouth; [if] that he is far away, he indulges in bad words. [If] he meets the enemy, he kneels down terrified on the road. [But after] arriving home, he says arrogant words."	玄云拙冤惡惶家 談智遙語跪説 寶口觀至途大藏伏施敵到言
gemu sūweni gesengge be henduhebi kai:	All these words apply to you.	These words apply exactly to you.	正也 爾 之謂
abka wakalabi ba na **74** gaibume tūmen tūmen cooha wabuci geli amba gisun gisurerengge dere ainu kirirakō: abka de ainu gelerakō:	How can you use arrogant words, since Heaven disapproved you, took away [your] territories and caused one hubdred million soldiers to be killed: How unbearable should it be!	Heaven disapproved of you, took away your territories and caused one million soldiers all to be killed: how [is it possible] to use arrogant words!	蒼失百皆**22b**言羞天 天其萬被尚何何也 怪土兵殺説不不地馬死大自畏 言不畏天

	How are you not afraid of Heaven?	How do you not feel ashamed, how are you not afraid of Heaven?	
ŷai-a niẙalma endebuhe ba be bahanabi: bi waka mujangga seme alime gaibi: beẙe be beẙe kiribure: ūile be tūc̣ibubi būre oc̣i: tere ūjui sain niẙalma: tenteke niẙalma be abka inu 75 saiŝambi: niẙalma inu ūrušebi ūrgunjembǐ:	Every man can make mistakes; I too have to confess mistakes and I have to take the blame; but if a mistake is made and repented [?], then the man is a very good one. Heaven too praises such a man, and the man too will act well and be glad.	From the Son of Heaven till the common people, everybody can make mistakes. If one is able to be conscious of [his] mistakes and confesses the fault, if he repents and accepts the responsibility [for it], if he corrects the mistake, then he is a very good man. Heaven too will love him, and the man too will be glad.	但以凡能過是責過好愛喜 自至有自即自贖乃之 天庶過知認悔其上人 子人怨其不自罪等亦 也
beẙei waka be bahanabi: beẙe tuc̣iburakō: mini ūile be geren šūwa ŝa serengge dulimbai niẙalma:	Since I myself made mistakes, I cannot elevate myself [above other men]; all the people call my faults a "gentle rustling" [provoked] by a man of the middle.	Since [my] own mistakes are known, I cannot elevate myself [above other men]; I only wait for the people's words, as a man of the middle.	若不只乃 知能待中 其自人等 過舉言人
waka be mūrime ūru arame gisurerengge tere enteheme dūbei niẙalma: tenteke niẙalma be: niẙalma inu ibiẙ[a]mbi: abka inu wakalambi:	If one says that a fault is distored and transforms it into a good thing, then that man will forever be considered the lowest of the low. People will detest such a man too. Heaven too will disapprove him.	If a man does not confess his fault and insists on transforming a bad thing into a good one, then he is an inferior man, Heaven would disapprove him, people too would detest him. This is a self-evident rule.	不強是等怪惡然 認自等人之之之 其非乃下人是自 過為人天亦自理也 **23a** 也
		Please report this to [your] superiors!	請詳之

Comment

The content of the Manchu text of this section could be regarded as constituting something of a "résumé". However, the text is difficult to understand in some cases – as for instance in the reference to "Soosida-i bithe" (i.e. *Xuantan baozang* 玄談寶藏 in the Chinese version), for which we were unable to find any information in the sources at our disposition.

The Chinese text only ends with the invitation to the reader to "report this to the superiors". This request justifies the definition of "proclamation to the Ming", which was probably created in order to undermine the Chinese officials' fighting morale. A Manchu translation of this exhortation was obviously not needed.

[Conclusions]

○ hadai gūrun-i efujehe onggolo: suwayan **76** indahōn aniya: birgan de senggi eyehe: tuttu ganio joribi jurcehekō hadai gūrun efujehe:

jai yehei gūrun-i efujere onggolo: šanggiyan ihan aniya hacin hacin-i ūsei aga agaha: fulgiyan mūduri aniya senggi aga agaha: tuttu ganio joribi jurcehekō yehei gūrun efujehe:

nikan sini bejing hecen-i bira de **77** juwe aniya senggi eyehe ganio jurcembio atanggi bicibe isimbi kai:

mini gūrun de fulgiyan bonio aniya: fulgiyan mūduri aniya: juwe aniya hibsui aga agaha: tere abka inu gosire be sakini seme agahangge kai:

Before the Hada state was destroyed, in the year of the yellow dog, blood flowed in the rivers. This omen was shown but did not lead to any change, and the Hada state was destroyed.

Furthermore, before the Yehe state was destroyed, many kinds of seeds rained down in the year of the white ox; in the year of the red dragon blood rained. These omens were shown [but] not recognized, and the Yehe state was destroyed.

Oh Chinese, in the river of your city of Beijing blood flowed in two years; this omen was not recognized. No matter when, something will happen.

In two years, the year of the red monkey and the year of the red dragon, in my realm honey was raining. Heaven sent this rain [tacitly] saying: "take cognizance of [my] love!"

The [state of the] Southern Pass was destroyed; before that, in the *wu-xu* year bloody water flowed in the rivers. No attention was paid to Heaven's omen, and this led to the destruction of the state.

The [state of the] Northern Pass was destroyed; before that, many kinds of seeds rained down in the *xin-chou* year. In the *wu-shen* year blood rained.

No attention was paid to Heaven's omens, and this, in the end, led to the destruction of the state.

Now, in the Yu River of your Southern Dynasty's Beijing, blood flowed in two years. Heaven sent down these omens, which in the end would cause something to happen.

In two years, the *bing-shen* year and the *bing-chen* year, Heaven sent down honey-rain in my realm.

How did you not understand the good omens of sweet dew shown by Heaven, [which reveals that] it is tacitly on my side!

南關之亡也先於戊戌年河流血水天兆不違遂致國亡

北關之亡也先於辛丑年雨各色種戊申年雨血

天兆不違終致國亡

今你南朝北京玉河兩年流23b血天降兆終須至矣

我國中丙申及丙辰兩年天降蜜雨

豈非天示甘露之瑞而默祐我乎

Conclusions

Manchu	English (1)	English (2)	Chinese
nikan simbe abka wakalabi hacin hacin-i ganio jorire:	Oh Chinese, Heaven disapproved of you and showed all kinds of omens.	Heaven disapproves of your Southern Dynasty and often inflicted misfortune on you.	天怪你南 朝屢降災 異
cooha wabure ba na gaibure oci: beÿei waka be sarkō geli mini gūrun amban cooha geren seme kemuni amba gisun gisurerengge nikan si abka de eljerengge kai ·:·	While [your] soldiers are killed and [your] territories are lost, [you say that] you are not aware of your personal faults. On the contrary, you use arrogant words saying "my Empire is great, the soldiers are numerous." Oh Chinese, you are acting in opposition to Heaven!	While [your] soldiers are killed and [your] territories are lost, [you say that] you are not aware of your personal faults. On the contrary, you use arrogant words saying that your Empire is great, the soldiers are strong. In this way you are in opposition to Heaven!	兵將敗死 地土失守 而不知自 咎復說國 大兵眾大 言大語是 乃抗天也

Comment

This last section gives the impression of having been added the last moment. The real and logical conclusion is rather to be found in the previous section, which ends with the exhortation to make this proclamation known to Chinese "superiors". The correct dates for when blood flowed in a river, announcing the Hada's annihilation (1598) according to the sexagenary cycle, and the good omens of "honey rain"[1] (1596 and 1616), contrast with the wrong cycle-dates for seed- und blood-rain announcing the Yehe's annihilation in 1619. For the first of these omens, the Manchu text gives the not-existing cycling combination *šanggiyan ihan*, which corresponds in the Chinese text to the *xinchou* 辛丑 combination. This date refers to 1601 and is clearly too early for an event which happened in 1619.

---

[1] Honey-rain is mentioned twice in the *JMZD*: on the 24th day of the 4th month (of 1617 = 28th May) a honey rain "rained" (*hibsu aga agaha*) in 700 places (I, 161). The same phenomenon happened also one year before (*JMZD* I, 69), and "rain" was so abbundant that Nurhaci "licked it [from the leaves] and, since it was tasty, he let all the princes and dignitaries lick it saying 'lick it'" (*han ileme tuwafi. ere sain ningge. beise ambasa gemu ile seme ilebuhe*). A third "honey-rain" is mentioned in ms. Guimet 61625, giving the date *fulgiyan tasha aniya, ninggun biyai ice de* = 1st of the 6th month of the red-tiger-year = 24 June 1626 (see Pang/Stary, p. 45). It is missing in the *JMZD*.

Abbreviations and works cited

Chan, Hok-lam: *Legitimation in Imperial China. Discussion under the Jurchen-Chin Dynasty (1115-1234)*. Seattle-London 1984.

Chan, Hok-lam: "Calamities and Government Relief under the Jurchen". *Papers on Society and Culture in Early Modern China*. Taipei 1992, pp. 781-872.

Chavannes, É.: *Les Mémoires Historiques de Se-ma Ts'ien*, I-VI. Leiden 1967-1969.

De Groot, J. J. M.: *Universismus*. Berlin 1918.

De Groot, J. J. M.: *The Religious System of China*, I-VI. Leiden 1892-1910, Taipei 1976².

De Harlez, C.: *Histoire de l'Empire de Kin ou Empire d'Or Aisin gurun-i suduri bithe*. Louvain 1887, New York 1979².

De Woskin, K., – J. I. Crump Jr.: *In Search of the Supernatural*. Stanford 1996.

Franke, H.: "Treaties Between Sung and Chin". *Études Song in Memoriam Étienne Balazs*, ed. F. Aubin. Paris 1970, pp. 55-84.

Franke, H.: "Chinese Texts on the Jurchen. A Translation of the Jurchen Monograph in the San-ch'ao pei-meng hui-pien". *Zentralasiatische Studien* 9 (1975), pp. 119-186.

Franke, H.: "Chinese Texts on the Jurchen II. A Translation of Chapter One of the Chin-shih". *Zentralasiatische Studien* 12 (1978), pp. 413-452.

Franke, H.: "The Chin Dynasty". *The Cambridge History of China*, 6: *Alien regimes and border states, 907-1368*, ed. H. Franke and D. Twitchett. Cambridge 1994, pp. 215-320.

Franke, O.: *Geschichte des chinesischen Reiches*, I: Berlin 1965². II-III: Berlin 1961². IV: Berlin 1948. V: Berlin 1952.

Franke & Chan: Herbert Franke and Hok-lam Chan: *Studies on the Jurchens and the Chin Dynasty*. Aldershot 1997.

Fuchs, W.: *Beiträge zur Mandjurischen Bibliographie und Literatur*. Tôkyô 1936.

Fuchs, W.: "Neue Beiträge zur mandjurischen Bibliographie und Literatur". *Monumenta Serica* VII (1942), pp. 1-37.

Gibert, L.: *Dictionnaire historique et géographique de la Mandchourie*. Hongkong 1934.

Haenisch, E.: *Zum Untergang zweier Reiche. Berichte von Augenzeugen aus den Jahren 1232-33 und 1368-70*. Wiesbaden 1969 (Abhandlungen für die Kunde des Morgenlandes XXXVIII/4).

Hauer, E.: *Huang-Ts'ing K'ai-kuo Fang-lüeh. Die Gründung des mandschurischen Kaiserreiches*. Berlin-Leipzig 1926.

Hummel, A. W. (ed.): *Eminent Chinese of the Ch'ing Period (1644-1912)*, I-II. Washington 1943-1944.

Imanishi Shunjū 今西春秋: "«Kō Kin geki Min Banreki kōtei bun» ni tsuite" 《後金檄明萬曆皇帝文》について. *Chōsen gakuhō* 朝鮮學報 67 (1973), pp. 137-158.

Imanishi Shunju: "Über einen Aufruf der Späteren Chin an die Ming von ca. 1623". *Oriens Extremus* 20 (1973), pp. 27-37.

JMZD: *Jiu Manzhou dang* 舊滿洲檔, ed. Ch'en Chieh-hsien 陳捷先, I-X. Taipei 1969.

Kopsch, H.: "Pao-sze. The Cleopatra of China". *China Review* IV (1875/76).

"Lao Manwen shangyu" 老滿文上諭. *Wenxian congbian* 文獻叢編 2 (1937); repr. Taipei 1964, vol. 上, p. 82; vol. 下, pp. 1053-1054.

Laričev, V. E.: *Istorija Zolotoj Imperii / The History of the Golden Empire*. Novosibirsk 1998.

Maljavkin: A. G.: "Czin'-ši. Glava 1-ja, perevod s kitajskogo". *Sbornik naučnych rabot prževal'cev*, Harbin 1942, pp. 1-58.

Manzhou shilu 滿洲實錄. First trilingual ed., Tōkyō 1937.

Manzhou yuanliu kao 满州源流考, ed. Sun Wenliang 孙文良 et al. Shenyang 1988.

Martynov, A. M. - T. A. Pang: "About Ideology of the Early Qing Dynasty". *Archiv Orientální* 71 (2003), pp. 385-394.

Matsui, H.: "Das Verwaltungsgebiet des Chin-Reiches in der Mandschurei". *Beiträge zur historischen Geographie der Mandschurei*, II. Ed. H. Matsui, W. Yanai, I. Inaba. Tōkyō 1912, pp. 115-205.

Matsui, H.: "Über die [sic] Verwaltungsgebiet des P'o-hai Reichs". *Beiträge zur historischen Geographie der Mandschurei*, I. Ed. W. Yanai, I. Inaba, H. Matsui Tōkyō 1914, pp. 338-370.

Matsumura Jun 松村潤: *Sin Taiso jitsuroku no kenkyū* 清太祖實錄の研究, Tōkyō 2001. (Tōhogaku Ajia bunken kenkyū sōkan 東北アヅア文獻研究叢刊 2).

Miranda, M.: "Das Dongyi Nurhaci kao". *Materialien zur Vorgeschichte der Qing-Dynastie*, ed. G. Stary. Wiesbaden 1996, pp. 57-63.

MWLD: *Manwen laodang* 满文老檔 / *Tongki fuka sindaha hergen-i dangse* / *Secret Chronicles of the Manchu Dynasty*, I-VII. Translated and edited by N. Kanda et al., Tōkyō 1955-1963.

Pan Zhe 潘喆, Sun Fangming 孙方明, Li Hongbin 李鸿彬 (eds.): *Qing ruguan qian shiliao xuanji* 清入关前史料选辑, I. Beijing 1984, pp. 289-196.

Pang, T. A.: "The Manchu script reform of 1632: New data and new questions". *Writings in the Altaic World*, ed. J. Janhunen & V. Rybatzki. Helsinki 1999, pp. 201-206.

Pang, T. A.: "Nachodka konca XX veka: samyj rannij man'čžrskij ksilograf". *Altaica* 4 (2000), pp. 91-100.

Pang/Stary: Tatiana A. Pang – Giovanni Stary: *New Light on Manchu Historiography and Literature*. Wiesbaden 1998.

Pang Xiaomei 庞晓梅: "The Manchu-Chinese text of the «Proclamation of Nurhaci to the Ming»: What version was written first?". *Qingshi lunji. Qinghe Wang Zhonghan jiaoshou jiushi huadan* 清史论集. 庆贺王锺翰教授九十华诞, ed. Zhu Chengru 朱诚如. Beijing 2003, pp. 709-714.

Pang Xiaomei 庞晓梅 – G. Sidali [Stary] 斯达理: "Zui zhongyao kexue faxian zhi yi: Lao Manwen xie de «Hou Jin xi Ming Wanli huangdi wen»" 最重要科学发现之一: 老满写的《后金檄明万历皇帝文》. *Manxue yanjiu* 满学研究 6, ed. Yan Chongnian 阎崇年, Beijing 2000, pp. 186-191.

Qiao Zhizhong 乔治忠: "«Hou Jin xi Ming Wanli huangdi wen» kaoxi" 《后金檄明万历皇帝文》考析. *Qingshi yanjiu* 清史研究 3 (1992), pp. 106-110.

Reckel, J.: *Bohai*. Wiesbaden 1995 (Aetas Manjurica 5).

Roth Li, G.: "State Building before 1644". *The Cambridge History of China*, Vol. 9/1: *The Qing Empire to 1800*. Ed. W. J. Peterson, Cambridge 2002, pp. 9-72.

Sagang Sečen: *Geschichte der Mongolen und ihres Fürstenhauses*. Herausgegeben und mit einem Nachwort von Walther Heissig, Zürich 1985. [Rep. of I. J. Schmidt's translation, St. Petersburg-Leipzig 1829].

Sekai bunkashi daikei 世界文化史大系, 19, Tōkyō 1938.

Song Dexuan 宋德宣: *Manzu zhexue sixiang yanjiu* 满族哲学思想研究. Shenyang 1994, pp. 109-120.

Stary, G.: "La politica mancese delle 'sette accuse': Una costante per giustificare la conquista della Cina e della Corea". *Studi in onore di Mario Grignaschi*. Ed. G. Bellingeri & G. Vercellin. Venezia 1988, pp. 43-55. (Eurasiatica 5: Quaderni del Dipartimento di Studi Eurasiatici, Università degli Studi di Venezia).

Stary, G.: "Some Preliminary Remarks on the Authenticity and Historical Value of Qing Taizu Nurhaci's 'Holy Teachings' (The Manchu Version – *Enduringge Tacihiyan*)". *Central Asiatic Journal* 49/1 (2005), pp. 60-70.

Taylor, R.: "Kuo Tzu-hsing". *Dictionary of Ming Biography 1368-1644*, I. Ed. L. C. Goodrich. New York-London 1976.

Thiele, D.: *Der Abschluss eines Vertrages: Diplomatie zwischen Sung- und Chin-Dynastie 1117-1123*. Wiesbaden 1971.

Von Mende, E.: *China und die Staaten auf der koreanischen Halbinsel bis zum 12. Jh.* Wiesbaden 1982. (Sinologica Coloniensia 11).

Weiers, M.: "Zur Registratur der mandschurischen Holztäfelchen über Ajiges Invasion der Ming im Jahre 1636". *Aetas Manjurica* 6, ed. M. Gimm. G. Stary, M. Weiers. Wiesbaden 1998, pp. 251-314.

Weiers, M.: "Ein Blockdrucktext betreffend die orthographische Präzisierung der Buchstaben ohne Punkte und Kreise durch Dahai". *Zentralasiatische Studien* 29 (1999), pp. 87-96.

Weiers, M.: "Einige Bemerkungen zur Geschichte der Entwicklung der mandschurischen Schrift". *Acta Orientalia Academiae Scientiarum Hungaricae* 55/1-3 (2002), pp. 269-279.

Werner, E. T. C.: *A Dictionary of Chinese Mythology*. New York 1961.

Wittfogel, K. A. – Fêng Chia-shêng: History of Chinese Society Liao (907-1125). Philadelphia 1949.

Zhang Yuxing 张玉兴 et al.: *Aixin Jueluo jiazu quanshu* 爱新觉罗家族全书. Jilin 1997, vol. 7, pp. 36-37.